Book 2
Identity and Expression

Edited by Philip Seargeant

This publication forms part of the Open University module A150 *Voices and texts*. Details of this and other Open University modules can be obtained from the Student Registration and Enquiry Service, The Open University, PO Box 197, Milton Keynes MK7 6BJ, United Kingdom (tel. +44 (0)845 300 60 90; email general-enquiries@open.ac.uk).

Alternatively, you may visit the Open University website at www.open.ac.uk where you can learn more about the wide range of modules and packs offered at all levels by The Open University.

To purchase a selection of Open University materials visit www.ouw.co.uk, or contact Open University Worldwide, Walton Hall, Milton Keynes MK7 6AA, United Kingdom for a brochure (tel. +44 (0)1908 858793; fax +44 (0) 1908 858787; email ouw-customer-services@open.ac.uk).

The Open University Walton Hall, Milton Keynes MK7 6AA

First published 2010

Edited and designed by The Open University.

Printed and bound in the United Kingdom by Bell & Bain Ltd, Glasgow.

ISBN 978 1 8487 3377 0

1.1

Contents

Introduction

Philip Seargeant

Contents

Disciplines and approaches

The central topics of Book 2 are *language* and *writing*. These are both essential elements in the creation of texts. Language is the raw material from which all the texts we have looked at so far are constructed. Some of them also include music or dramatic action, but central to them all is the careful manipulation of language. And writing is the process by which this raw material is converted into coherent works of cultural expression. It is the creative act that turns words and ideas into texts.

With these two elements as its main focus, the approach of this book is slightly different from that of the previous one. Rather than engaging in the analysis of a selection of pre-existing texts – and examining the interplay of voices that comprise them – we'll be looking instead at the fundamental ingredients of any act of verbal composition, and at how these ingredients can be combined in acts of expression. In other words we take a slight step back in this book, and rather than looking primarily at the *products* of textual composition, we look instead at the *resources* and *processes* that are involved in that composition.

Before outlining the nature of these resources and processes in more detail, let's briefly review the approach we took in Book 1. In Book 1 we examined a selection of important and influential texts that were written at various historical times and for a variety of cultural purposes. We looked at classical texts, at religious texts, at poetic and dramatic texts, and at compositions that combine words and music. In each case our analysis involved an examination of the context in which the texts were written, the structure of their composition, and the influence they have had on readers and audiences at various times and places throughout history. Depending on the purpose for which these different texts were written and the generic structure they took, we looked at them from the perspective of different *academic disciplines*. Each of these academic disciplines (Classical Studies, Religious Studies, Literature and Music) offered a specific way of highlighting certain important features or qualities of the texts we looked at, and gave us a theoretical framework with which to analyse them. This analysis then helped us to understand something of the significance that each text had for the readership and audience it was composed for, and of the ways in which subsequent generations and different cultures have also interpreted it. In summary, the previous book followed an approach centred on the textual analysis of a selection of notable cultural artefacts; and in this way it highlighted the important role that texts play as a means of cultural expression.

The shape of Book 2

In Book 2 we continue the examination of the ways in which texts operate as a means of cultural expression, but rather than focusing on a selection of pre-existing texts and analysing their cultural significance, instead we'll examine two fundamental elements in the act of composition. To this end, Chapters 1 and 2 have as their focus the study of language, and Chapters 3 and 4 look at the process of writing. In doing this, the book divides broadly into two parts, with each part exploring ideas from two further academic disciplines: those of English Language Studies and Creative Writing.

Language Studies – or, as the discipline is often more formally known, Linguistics – has as its main focus the theoretical analysis of human language and language use. In other words, it looks at how languages are structured, what they are used for, and how they have evolved. For many people, language is considered an essential element of what it means to be human. For example, the Renaissance dramatist Ben Jonson wrote that language is 'the only benefit man hath to expresse his excellencie of mind above other creatures' (1947 [1641], pp. 620–1). Given the important and complex role that language plays in the human experience, the discipline of Linguistics is naturally a very broad one. For our purposes, we'll concentrate primarily on the ways in which language functions as a fundamental resource by means of which people express their ideas and identities, and through which they interact with the social world around them. In Chapters 1 and 2 we'll look at the use of language (and specifically the English language) in the creation of texts and communicative acts in a variety of different contexts, and consider the range of ways that language gives us for expressing our experience of the world. We'll look at examples from everyday language use, as well as from the media and literature. As language is the raw material from which all texts are built, it pays to have an understanding of its nature and workings – and so this is what we'll focus on in the first half of the book.

The second half moves to the discipline of Creative Writing. This is a relatively new academic discipline at university level. That is, although people have engaged in acts of creative writing since the beginning of human civilisation (in Book 1, for example, we looked at a text, Homer's *Iliad*, dating back almost three thousand years), only in the last thirty years or so has it been regularly taught as a distinct university subject. As an activity, though, writing is central to our social existence.

So many aspects of our everyday life involve some sort of writing, be it scribbling out a shopping list, sending emails, or working on an assignment. In this respect we are all already 'writers'.

Creative writing is, of course, a slightly different type of writing to most of the writing we all engage in on a daily basis. It's one that draws on the imagination and that uses structures and strategies to engage the imagination of a reader. It might well be that, in studying A150 *Voices and texts*, you don't feel you have any particular ambition to become a published creative writer yourself. But training yourself in the techniques and strategies of writing is not the only benefit to be had from studying Creative Writing. Looking at the processes involved in writing gives an insightful perspective into the nature of other people's texts. In effect, the discipline of Creative Writing allows us to consider the text not solely from the point of view of the reader or audience – as we did in Book 1 – but also from that of the writer. So even if you don't have any specific ambitions to develop skills in this area, you'll find that the opportunity to think from this perspective, and to engage with the processes involved in the creation of texts, will provide insights into what goes into the creation of the sort of cultural artefacts that we examined in Book 1. In Chapters 3 and 4 of the book, therefore, you'll have the opportunity to explore and experiment with a number of creative writing strategies, and to engage in the crafting of language to create short pieces of both prose and poetry.

Given the different focuses that the two disciplines have, there is also an inherent difference in what is involved in studying them. You'll see this most noticeably in the different types of activities you are asked to do. In the English Language Studies chapters, the focus is more on the analysis of extracts of speech and writing, and the activities involve skills such as close reading and critical analysis. In the Creative Writing chapters, the focus is more on developing practical skills, and the activities are thus more practice-oriented and include tasks involving editing and the composition of short texts.

While the book is structured in two parts around the two disciplines, however, there is also a great deal of common ground between them. Although Language Studies conventionally tends to analyse other people's language use and Creative Writing tends to play with a person's own use of language, they should not be seen as mutually exclusive. Throughout the book we'll be making links between the two, and aiming to explore how approaching a text from both a critical and a creative perspective can help us appreciate the way that we actively engage with words whenever we use language.

In summary, then, the approaches in this book – which focus on the language from which texts are assembled and the writing processes by which they're composed – are a complement to the textual analysis that we undertook in Book 1, and to which we'll return in Book 3. In Book 2, the focus is less on the interpretation of texts, and more on the act of their composition. But this approach shares with the earlier approach the same interest in the place that the production and consumption of texts has in the way human civilisation organises itself. It shares the same desire to understand the way that meaning is made by the artful manipulation of language. For if language is 'the only benefit man hath to expresse his excellencie of mind above other creatures', it is in the composition of culturally resonant texts that this benefit is most fully realised – and this book will take a closer look at exactly what is involved in this composition, and at how we shape language to express ourselves.

Reference

Jonson, B. (1947 [1641]) 'Timber: or, Discoveries' in Herford, C.H. and Simpson, P. (eds) *The Works of Ben Jonson*, vol. 8, Oxford, Clarendon Press.

1 Speech and dialect

Philip Seargeant

Contents

Aims

This chapter will:

- introduce you to the diversity of spoken language, and the way this diversity is used as a marker of identity
- explore the concepts of 'accent' and 'dialect'
- examine the difference between 'standard' and 'non-standard' English, and the ways in which people evaluate the speech of others with reference to these concepts.

Materials you will need

- DVD 2 (audio)

Introduction: the study of language in use

This chapter and the next have language itself as their main focus. We'll be looking at ways in which we can analyse language – and specifically the English language – and at how people use English as part of everyday life. As noted in the Introduction, language is an intrinsic part of human experience, and because of this, it can be studied from a great number of different perspectives. The study of language includes such diverse issues as:

- the structure of languages – that is, the specific grammatical rules that govern the composition of sentences in different languages
- how the brain processes language – in other words, what goes on inside your brain when you use language
- how people acquire languages – either learning them from infancy, or studying them later in life
- how language is used for creative or persuasive purposes, as, for example, in the composition of poetry or public speeches.

Each of these perspectives is a branch of the general discipline of **Linguistics**. In Chapters 1 and 2, however, we'll be looking predominantly at the way people *use* language, and at how that usage is influenced by the society they live in and the social interactions they take part in. This approach to the study of language is known broadly as **sociolinguistics**. The focus here is on the relationship between language use and social structures. It's an approach that examines the ways in which people use language, what they use it for, and how this use is influenced by their social circumstances and environment. If this all sounds rather abstract and theoretical to you at the moment, don't worry because we'll be looking at several examples of actual language use, and will be discussing exactly what the relationship is between language and society, as we progress through the first half of the book.

Let's begin by making a simple but fundamental point. When we speak we communicate both by what we say (the content of our **utterances**) and by how we say it (the form those utterances take). As soon as someone speaks even a couple of words to us, we begin to make judgements about their identity – where they are from, what sort of education they have had, what their social background is, and so on. This first chapter will examine what it is about the way we speak that

[handwritten margin notes:]
the term used for the general study of language

Examines the relationship between language and social life

A complete unit of speech used by someone

allows people to infer all this information. In other words, we'll be looking at how our use of language is influenced by the environment from which we come or in which we live (that is, our social surroundings), and how important this context is for the way that we communicate with each other.

A note on terminology

The word 'utterance' in this context simply means a complete unit of speech that someone uses when speaking. It will often be preceded and followed by a space of silence, or by a change of speaker. It could be a whole sentence, a string of sentences, or just a single word ('Help' or 'no'), or possibly even a half-spoken word or meaningful sound ('Erm …'). As you can see, this meaning is slightly different from the colloquial use of the word.

As with most disciplines, Linguistics uses several technical terms, and this is one of them. These technical terms help to describe in a detailed and exact way the phenomena that Linguistics studies. In this book, as in all the others, there is a glossary at the end which has a list of definitions of all the words that are highlighted in bold. As was noted in the Study Companion, you don't need to memorise all these definitions, but as you encounter them it's worth thinking about the particular meaning they have as technical terms, as this will help you understand the ideas they are being used to represent.

— sequences of connected speech or writing, usually made up of more than one sentence

As the title of this first chapter suggests, we'll be looking predominantly at examples from spoken **discourse** here, while in Chapter 2 we'll look more at the written use of language. There is another difference of focus between the two chapters. In this first chapter we'll be looking predominantly at **dialect** – that is, language as it is defined by its *users*. In Chapter 2 we'll look at register – that is, language as it is defined by its *uses*. (The significance of this distinction will be explained in greater detail below.) The use of dialect is most noticeable in spoken language, but it also exists in written language; while the use of register occurs in both spoken and written language. And although the titles of the chapters suggest a clear delineation between the different types of language use, in actual fact things are not nearly this clear-cut. After all, despite the fact I've just stated that this chapter will be focusing predominantly on spoken language, what you have in front of you is a book consisting entirely of writing (plus the occasional image). So even

The word 'discourse' was discussed briefly in the Study Companion. In the present context, it simply means a sequence of connected speech or writing. 'Utterance', which you encountered above, usually refers only to speech, and so 'discourse' is the more general term.

before we start, we are confronted with the paradox that the examples about the spoken form of the language will be represented in the book by means of the written language! (There are audio examples on DVD 2, of course, so you'll get the chance to listen to and analyse some actual speech a little later.)

What does it mean, then, to say that something that is very obviously a line of squiggles printed on a piece of paper (i.e. is very clearly 'writing') is an example of 'spoken' language? The answer concerns the fact that the way people *structure* what they write or say is an integral part of the communicative message they convey. Spoken language often has a distinctively different structure from written language. Likewise, a dialect that is spoken in one part of the UK will have a different internal structure to that spoken in another part. How people structure language in different ways is a complex and multifaceted process, yet it's something that happens automatically (and often unconsciously) in any instance of communication, and that is picked up on instantly by recipients of the message. These first two chapters will introduce you to some of this complexity, and to the crucial roles that language plays in our everyday lives as social beings.

1.1 Diversity and identity

Activity

Look at the three short utterances below. Each is a different way of saying 'Thank you'. Based solely on these simple phrases, what assumptions can you make about the type of people who might use them? What age, or social or geographical background, do you think people using these different phrases might have?

(a) 'Thanks awfully'

(b) 'Cheers mate'

(c) 'Ta love'.

Discussion

This is, of course, a rather speculative exercise. But to me, Example (a) sounds like the sort of thing that is likely to be used by someone from an upper middle class background, and probably from an older generation. Example (b) has a younger feel to it. I wouldn't associate it with any particular class, but it sounds colloquial, and possibly suggests a male rather than a female speaker. Example (c) has associations with the north of England for me. Again, there is a colloquial feel to it, and if I had to guess, I'd say this person was probably from a lower middle or working class background. All three have quite a British ring to them, though Example (b) could possibly also be used by someone from Australia or New Zealand.

As I say, this is hardly a scientific exercise. But the point to note is that even from simple two-word utterances like these we can make basic assumptions about the type of people who might use them. Each of these phrases has the same function – they are all expressions of gratitude – and yet they each consist of a different combination of words. And it is because of this combination of words that we are able to infer a meaning both about what the speaker was trying to express (a sense of gratitude), and about their identity.

Central to the study of sociolinguistics is what is known as **language variation**. This is the principle that the language people speak is variable – that the way it sounds and the way it is structured will vary depending on the person using it and the circumstances in which it is used. As you can see from the activity above, it is possible to make some rough inferences about a person's identity from even the most

the way in which forms and structures of language vary according to its users e. the circumstances in which it is used

9

basic evidence of their linguistic habits. And the reason we are able to do this is because people don't all use language the same way. We often talk of 'English' as a single entity. In sentences such as 'English is my native language', or '*Hard Times* is a novel written in English' or 'She's been learning English for five years now', we refer simply to a general concept called 'English'. But when we start to look at the language closely, and to examine in detail how people use it, we begin to see that there is a vast amount of diversity on display. Far from being one unchanging system, which everyone who speaks the language has knowledge of and access to in equal measure, English as it is actually used represents a bewilderingly wide range of different forms and incarnations. So, for example, the 'English' that I speak is different from the English in a Charles Dickens novel, or from that spoken by a university student studying the language in Beijing. Examples from all three would still be very recognisably 'English'; but at the same time, they would be distinct enough for us to start noticing patterns in their usage which could be used to differentiate between them.

This diversity in the language occurs on a number of different levels. Part of it happens on an entirely individual basis. When we speak or write we make sounds in the airwaves or marks on a piece of paper that are unique to us. For this reason, it is possible to recognise someone who you know well simply from the sound of their voice or the shape of their handwriting. In this respect, the sound of their voice is as unique to them as their facial features, and their handwriting is as much a part of them as their mannerisms or posture. But this individuality in language use is not restricted to the physical means used to produce speech or writing. It is also possible to recognise someone you know well from their turn of phrase or from particular expressions they favour. In other words, the way an individual organises the words and phrases he or she uses is also distinct, and everyone does it slightly differently.

The distinct pattern of language use that is unique to an individual is known as an **idiolect**.

Just as we can recognise individuals from the distinctive way they use language, it is also possible to identify their relationship to wider groups within society by their use of language. This is because we often use language in a similar way to the people around us, and because different groups develop different patterns of usage. At the most noticeable level this happens in the way different *national* groups use different languages. So, for example, the French as a group use a different language from Italians. Several centuries ago, they spoke varieties of the same language (Latin), but as their group identities evolved – and as the politics of that region of continental Europe gradually changed – the single language slowly altered into separate languages, which now have different names and resemble each other only very slightly. And this same phenomenon happens on far smaller scales as well, and occurs within communities whose members nominally speak the same language. As a general principle, language variation occurs according to the different ways people are grouped in society. This may be according to their geographical location, to their social class, or to other factors such as their gender. In each case, the associations we have with the people around us are reflected in the way we use language, and this in turn becomes an aspect of our identity as part of that group.

1.2 Dialect and accent

Let's now look in more detail at two particular ways in which speech differs from group to group. The first of these is **accent**, which refers to the ways in which people pronounce the words they speak.

This activity should take you about 20–30 minutes.

Activity

Look at the five couplets below. They are all from poems written in English. Most are by well-known writers, while one is a traditional folk-rhyme. Take a moment to read them aloud and then jot down which of the lines rhyme when you speak them. If you have a chance to ask someone who has a different geographical background to you, get them to try the activity as well, and then compare your results.

Burns – Scottish

Wordsworth (Cumbria)

Kipling (Sussex)

Blake (London)

1   Put this hat on your head, it will keep your head warm;
    Take a sweet kiss, it will do you no harm.

2   The jay makes answer as the magpie chatters;
    And all the air is filled with pleasant noise of waters.

3   If they call you 'pretty maid', and chuck you 'neath the chin,
    Don't you tell where no one is, nor yet where no one's been!

4   He glows with all the spirit of the Bard,
    Fame, honest fame, his great, his dear reward.

5   My mother groaned, my father wept,
    Into the dangerous world I leapt.

Discussion

Depending on where you are from, you may have thought that one or maybe two of these rhyme but the others don't. For me, brought up in London and speaking with a standard south-east England accent, the only one which actually rhymes is Couplet 5. In all the other examples, the vowel sounds of the words at the end of each line are different. So, for example, although the words 'Bard' and 'reward' in Couplet 4 both end in '-ard', when I pronounce them the first is more of an 'ahh' sound, and the second more of an 'or' sound. This particular couplet is from a poem by Robert Burns (Figure 1.1) called 'The Brigs of Ayr', which is written in Scots, the language variety traditionally spoken in Lowland Scotland (Smith, 1996). Couplet 1 is from 'The Juniper Tree', a traditional children's folk-rhyme from the American Midwest – Eastern Illinois, to be precise (Van Doren, 1919). Couplet 2 is from a poem by William Wordsworth (Figure 1.2) called 'Resolution and Independence'. This is in a Cumbrian accent, reflecting the speech of the part of the country where Wordsworth was born and lived for much of his life. Couplet 3 is from a poem by Rudyard Kipling called 'A Smuggler's Song'; it's written in a Sussex dialect and is an imitation of the speech of the community along the south coast of England where smugglers operated. And, finally, Couplet 5 is from 'Infant Sorrow' by William Blake. Blake was born and lived his early life in London. This couplet rhymes in a standard British English accent.

You can hear these five couplets read in the accents in which they were written in 'Rhymes and regional accents' on DVD 2. As you listen to the poems, you may spot other words that are pronounced differently from the way you would normally pronounce them.

On DVD 2 you can also find recordings of the complete poems from which these couplets are taken.

Figure 1.1   Alexander Nasmyth, *Robbie Burns*, 1787, oil on canvas, 38 × 32 cm. Scottish National Portrait Gallery, Edinburgh. Photo: © The Bridgeman Art Library.

Figure 1.2   Benjamin Robert Haydon, *Portrait of William Wordsworth*, 1842, oil on canvas, 125 × 99 cm. National Portrait Gallery, London. Photo: © Giraudon/The Bridgeman Art Library.

Many people think that accents are what *other* people have. They believe that they speak their native language without any accent, and that theirs is the neutral, natural way to pronounce the language. But as the linguist John Esling (1998, p. 169) writes:

> The fact is that everyone has an accent. It tells other people who we are because it reflects the places we have been and the things we have done. But the construct of accent, like so many other things, is relative. We may only realise that others think we have an accent when we leave the place we came from and find ourselves among people who share a different background from our own, or when a newcomer to our local area stands out as having a distinctly different pronunciation from most of those in our group – that is, relative to us.

As the activity above shows, though, when different accents are placed side by side, it is quite clear that our own way of pronouncing words is only one of many alternatives. What the sociolinguistic study of language does is survey and describe different pronunciations by looking at the **phonology** of the language – that is, the way its system of sounds is organised (see the box below). Sociolinguists also observe how these differences form patterns in the way that particular groups speak, and they relate these patterns to a number of different social categories. The sociolinguist Peter Stockwell contends that 'Accent can often tell us where someone comes from, their age, gender, level of education, social class, wealth, how well-travelled they are, and whether they are emotionally attached to their home-town, job or political party' (2002, p. 7).

Phonology

Phonology is the term used for the study of the sound system of a language. As is often remarked upon, the relationship between the way that English is written and the way that it is pronounced is not always straightforward. English spelling doesn't systematically represent the sound of words; a fact that can cause a fair amount of difficulty for anyone trying to learn English as a foreign language. In many instances, the same sound can be represented by different combinations of letters (e.g. practi**c**e and practi**s**e), while conversely, the same letter or letters can be pronounced in a number of different ways (e.g. **ch**ord and **ch**ortle). And, as we have seen above, the same word can be pronounced in different ways in different accents.

Because of this, sociolinguists who wish to accurately represent spoken language use a specialised form of notation called the **International Phonetic Alphabet (IPA)**. The IPA uses symbols that each represent one fixed sound, so they can be used to accurately transcribe the way that any utterance actually sounds. We won't be using the IPA in this book because it provides a level of detail that is unnecessary for our present purposes. But it is worth remembering that the relationship between the conventional alphabet and the speech sounds of English is not one of exact and stable representation. We'll revisit this issue in Chapter 4 when we look at how the sounds of language can be manipulated for poetic purposes.

This activity should take you about 30–40 minutes.

Activity

1   Take a few moments to answer the following questions about your own accent. Do you think you speak English with a particular accent? In what circumstances do you most notice your accent? What do you think of your accent? Are you proud of it, or do you sometimes try to hide it?

2   Listen to 'Attitudes towards accents' on DVD 2. What can you say about people's attitudes toward their own accents?

Discussion

As you heard on DVD 2, people have differing feelings about their own accents, and some of these feelings are strongly held. For many, accent is related to identity because it represents the community from which they come or with which they associate. In other words, it can be a very important part of an individual's social identity in terms of the allegiances that person feels to particular groups or communities, and also in how he or she is perceived by other people.

'Dialect' is sometimes used to refer to pronunciation as well as vocabulary and grammar, as in Jonnie Robinson's definition in 'Attitudes towards accents' on DVD 2. More often, however, it refers only to variation in vocabulary and grammar, the two aspects of variation on which we will focus in this section.

We'll return later to the issue of how people evaluate other people's accents. Before doing so, let's look at the other major way in which language variation manifests itself. Whereas 'accent' refers specifically to the way people pronounce the language, 'dialect' refers to the patterns of variation in vocabulary and **grammar**. There are two broad types of dialect: regional and social. A regional dialect is the distinctive pattern of usage that occurs in a community located in a particular geographical location. A social dialect is a variety shared by people of the same class, social status or educational background. Often the two are combined. So, for example, a person can speak a working-class Cockney dialect – that is, speak in a way that is distinctive of working-class communities living in the London area.

I'll discuss the concept of 'standard' and 'non-standard' language in greater detail in Section 1.3 of this chapter.

In popular usage the word 'dialect' is often used to mean 'regional' or 'non-standard' dialect, and as such it can have pejorative connotations. A common assumption is that the **standard language** (i.e. the one used in the media, in education, and in most official contexts) is the *correct* version, and that other varieties are imperfect renditions of this. But in sociolinguistics, *any* variety of language is a dialect. In other words, just as we all have an accent, so we also all speak in a particular dialect. From a purely linguistic point of view, all dialects are equal. There is nothing in the way they are individually structured that makes one better or worse than another. They are simply different. From a *social* point of view, however, dialects are not all equal, and we'll look at why this is the case in Section 1.3. First, though, let's look at some examples of dialect features from around the English-speaking world.

Dialectal difference can be found in almost all aspects of the grammar and vocabulary of a language, including things such as word order, the way different tenses are formed in verbs, and the choice of vocabulary. We'll concentrate here on two particular areas: the use of pronouns and different vocabularies.

In modern standard English, the personal pronoun 'you' is used to refer to both single and plural subjects. If I say something like, 'Could you please come over here?' it's not possible from the grammar of the sentence alone to tell if I'm addressing one person or several. This was not always so. As is still the case in many European languages, English used to make a distinction here, with the word 'thou' used for the singular and 'you' for the plural. Over the centuries, though, this distinction slowly disappeared from standard English. 'You' began to be used both for the plural and as a polite term for referring to individual people – in the same way that 'vous' is in French – and gradually the polite form entirely replaced the basic singular 'thou' (Trudgill, 1999, p. 85).

In many regional English dialects, however, a distinction between the singular and plural is still made. In dialects around Liverpool and certain parts of the north-east of England, for example, the pronoun 'youse' (pronounced so as to rhyme with the verb 'use') will be used when referring to more than one person (see Table 1.1). In the southern states of the USA, the pronoun 'yall' is common, while in the Pittsburgh area of Philadelphia people use the pronoun 'yinz'. As Watson notes, while some people may consider these pronouns to be misuses of proper English and thus in some way inferior, 'the non-standard dialects are actually doing a "better job" here than the standard variety because they make a contrast, like many other European languages, which Standard English cannot without adding a phrase like *you guys*' (2009, p. 347).

Table 1.1 Plural second-person pronouns in English

	Standard English	Liverpool and the north-east of England	Southern US English	Pittsburgh
2nd person singular	Are you coming?	Are you coming?	Are you coming?	Are you coming?
2nd person plural	Are you coming?	Are youse coming?	Are yall coming?	Are yinz coming?

Source: Watson (2009, p. 347)

Another key area in which dialects differ is in terms of vocabulary. The dialect specialist Peter Trudgill gives the example of different words used across the UK for 'very' (1999, p. 104). So the phrase 'It's very tasty', could be spoken in the following different ways in different parts of the country:

It's *right* tasty (Central North)

It's *well* tasty (Home Counties)

It's *gey* tasty (Northumberland)

It's *gradely* tasty (Lancashire)

That's *wholly* tasty (Eastern Counties)

It be *main* tasty (Wiltshire and Hampshire)

This activity should take you about 20 minutes.

Activity

Read the following extracts from well-known works of literature, all of which use a specific dialect of English as a way of indicating something about the geographical or social milieu in which the characters live. As you read each extract, think about the following questions:

1 What particular aspects of the language appear to be non-standard dialect features?

2 Do any of these authors represent accent as well as dialect, and if so, how?

3 Do you have any idea of where these dialects are from?

Extract 1

I was powerful lazy and comfortable – didn't want to get up and cook breakfast. Well, I was dozing off again, when I thinks I hears a sounds of 'boom!' away up the river. I rouses up and rests on my elbow and listens; pretty soon I hears it again. I hopped up and went and looked out at a hole in the leaves, and I see a bunch of smoke laying on the water a long ways up – about abreast the ferry. And there was the ferry-boat full of people, floating along down. I knowed what was the matter, now. 'Boom!' I see the white smoke squirt out of the ferry-boat's side. You see, they was firing cannon over the water, trying to make my carcass come to the top.

[handwritten margin notes: – when is past tense pluralises – no accent! – location?]

Extract 2

(Village roadside. Martin is sitting near the forge, cutting sticks.)

TIMMY   Let you make haste out there. I'll be putting up new fires at the turn of day, and you haven't the half of them cut yet.

MARTIN   It's destroyed I'll be whacking your old thorns till the turn of day, and I with no food in my stomach would keep the life of a pig. Let you come out here and cut them yourself if you want them cut, for there's an hour every day when a man has a right to his rest.

TIMMY   Do you want me to be driving you off again to be walking the roads? There you are now, and I giving you your food, and a corner to sleep, and money with it; and, to hear the talk of you, you'd think I was after beating you, or stealing your gold.

[handwritten margin notes: – farming? Lincs?]

Extract 3

THE MAN   I'll tell you why. Fust: I'm intelligent – ff ff f! it's rotten cold here – yes: intelligent beyond the station o life into which it has pleased the capitalist to call me; and they dont like a man that sees through em. Second, an intelligent bein needs a doo share of appiness; so I drink something cruel when I get the chawnce. Third, I stand by my class and do as little as I can so's to leave arf the job for me fellow workers. Fourth, I'm fly enough to know wots inside the law and wots outside it; and inside it I do as the capitalists do: pinch what I can lay me hands on. In a proper state of society I am sober, industrious and honest: in Rome, so to speak, I do as the Romans do. Wots the consequence? When trade is bad – and it's rotten bad just now – and the employers az to sack arf their men, they generally start on me.

Discussion

Extract 1 is a passage from Mark Twain's *Huckleberry Finn* (1999 [1884], p. 35). In the preface to the novel, Twain writes that:

> In this book a number of dialects are used, to wit: the Missouri Negro dialect; the extremest form of the backwoods South-Western dialect; the ordinary 'Pike-County' dialect; and four modified variations of this last. The shadings have not been done in a haphazard fashion, or by guess-work; but painstakingly, and with the trustworthy guidance and support of personal familiarity with these several forms of speech.
>
> (Twain, 1999 [1884], p. 2)

In other words, although this is an artistic representation of dialect rather than a naturally occurring piece of discourse, Twain has attempted to accurately replicate features of the speech of the communities in which the novel is set. And he has done this both in terms of vocabulary choice and grammatical structure. A couple of features that you might have noticed in this passage are the use of the intensifier 'powerful' rather than 'very' in the phrase 'I was *powerful* lazy'; and the use of the non-standard verb form 'knowed' instead of 'knew' for the simple past tense in the phrase 'I *knowed* what was the matter'. Features such as these are part of the distinctive voice that the author creates for the narrator here.

Extract 2 is from a play called *The Well of the Saints* by the Irish dramatist J.M. Synge (1981 [1905], p. 147). The action of the play is set in rural County Wicklow in the east of Ireland, and there are a number of features of 'Irish English' in the characters' speech. One notable example here is the use of what is known as 'it-clefting'. This is a syntactic structure in which a single verb phrase is broken into two phrases by the addition of the word 'it' (Harris, 1993). In standard English, for example, we might say 'I'll be destroyed', but in this extract Martin says 'It's destroyed I'll be'. Another common feature in Irish English is the use of 'after' plus the '-ing' form of a verb as a way of indicating the immediate past (Hickey, 2007). This is used in the extract when Timmy says 'you'd think I was after beating you'. Again, features such as these contribute to the way that the characters' identities are represented.

Finally, Extract 3 is from George Bernard Shaw's play *Major Barbara* (1960 [1907], p. 76; Figure 1.3). The action in this scene is set in West Ham, in the East End of London. In this extract, Shaw is representing both a working-class East End dialect and an accent. He represents the

Figure 1.3   Clifford Williams's version of George Bernard Shaw's *Major Barbara* for the Royal Shakespeare Company at Aldwych Theatre, London, 1970. Photo: © Donald Cooper/Photostage.

accent by using non-standard spelling for many of the words the characters say. For example, when the man says 'an intelligent *bein* needs a *doo* share of *appiness*' the words that I've italicised are all items of vocabulary that occur in standard English, but the way they're pronounced (by dropping the 'g' from the end of 'going', writing 'doo' for 'due', and dropping the 'h' from the beginning of 'happiness') indicate a particular non-standard accent. Shaw also represents dialect features, for example, in the phrase 'leave arf the job for me fellow workers'. Here not only does the spelling again indicate the pronunciation of some of the words ('arf' for 'half'), but instead of the standard English possessive adjective 'my', the character uses the non-standard 'me' ('me fellow workers'). When the play is produced on the stage, the actor can supply the accent. But Shaw has made an effort to represent elements of the accent in the written text, possibly as an indicator for actors as to how to interpret the part, and also so that a reading public will be able to construct a mental image of how the man sounds.

Activity

Now listen to 'Writing in regional dialects' on DVD 2, in which the poets Valerie Bloom, W.N. Herbert and Ian McMillan talk about their own use of specific dialects and varieties of English in their writing. While listening, pay particular attention to what they say about the relationship between

This activity should take you about 30 minutes.

the type of language they use – both in their poetry and their everyday life – and issues of identity.

Discussion

For all three poets, the feelings they have about the variety of English spoken by the community in which they were brought up have a strong bearing on their own sense of identity. As Bloom says, 'It's really important for me to use my native language because the language is a part of the culture; it is a part of who I am. If you disregard a part of your culture, you're only half a person. And so to be complete, to be whole, I need to be able to express myself in the vehicle which my culture has given me.' Similar sentiments are echoed by both McMillan and Herbert. And all three then draw on the relationships between these dialects and the local culture in their composition of poetry.

All the extracts discussed above are in what are commonly called 'non-standard dialects'. If you look back at how I've described them, I've done so in contrast to a 'standard' English. The idea of standard English is a key concept in sociolinguistics. And one of the key reasons for this is because, when we evaluate different types of language use, we do so with reference to this notion of the standard. In the following section we'll look at this notion in more detail, and also at how and why people evaluate other people's language use.

1.3   Evaluating language

In the next activity you will read an extract from an essay called
'Mother tongue' by the Asian American novelist Amy Tan (Figure 1.4).
Tan was born and brought up in California; both her parents were
immigrants from China. As you'll see, this family background had an
influence on the linguistic environment in which she grew up and on
her own attitudes to language.

Figure 1.4   Amy Tan, 2007. Photographed by Mark Mainz. Photo: © Mark
Mainz/Getty Images for AFI.

This activity should
take you about
30–40 minutes.

Activity

Now turn to Reading 1.1 and read the extract from Tan's essay. In what ways do people pre-judge what others say according to the way they say it? How does this type of pre-judging result in a particular type of identity being imposed on Tan's mother?

Discussion

As Tan vividly relates, the way that her mother speaks English often gets in the way of what she wants to say. But this isn't because she is unable to express her ideas or wishes; it's because her audience often doesn't listen to the content of her speech because they are put off by the form it takes. She is what is commonly known as a 'non-native speaker'. That is, she learned the language later in her life, and because of this her accent and use of grammar are strongly influenced by her own native language. In the story about the gangster Du, for example, she uses a rather elliptical syntax and strings words together in an ungrammatical way. But, as the essay also observes, her competence in the language – especially in terms of her receptive understanding – is very good. Yet the perception of her communication skills by other people is often prejudiced by the type of English she speaks. In other words, people are quick to evaluate what she is saying on the basis of how she is saying it.

Tan's essay was originally presented as a talk as part of a panel entitled 'Englishes: whose English is it anyway?' at the State of the Language Symposium in San Francisco. The title of this panel reflects a debate about English which is attracting a lot of attention around the world at the moment. This is the issue of who *owns* English – that is, does English belong to some people, by virtue of their birth or upbringing, and does this then mean that these people have more right to decide what counts as correct English usage than others do?

At the end of the nineteenth century, Mark Twain asserted that '[t]here is no such thing as the Queen's English. The property has gone into the hands of a joint stock company and we [the United States] own the bulk of the shares' (Twain, 1989 [1897], p. 230). Over a century later, the centre of power has probably shifted even more emphatically towards the USA. Certainly, the population of the USA is far greater than that of the UK, so there is good reason to suggest that standard US English is the dominant model of English in the world today. But another shift has also taken place in the last few decades. English has now come to be a truly global language, and is spoken in areas all around the world (Figure 1.5). One of the consequences of this global

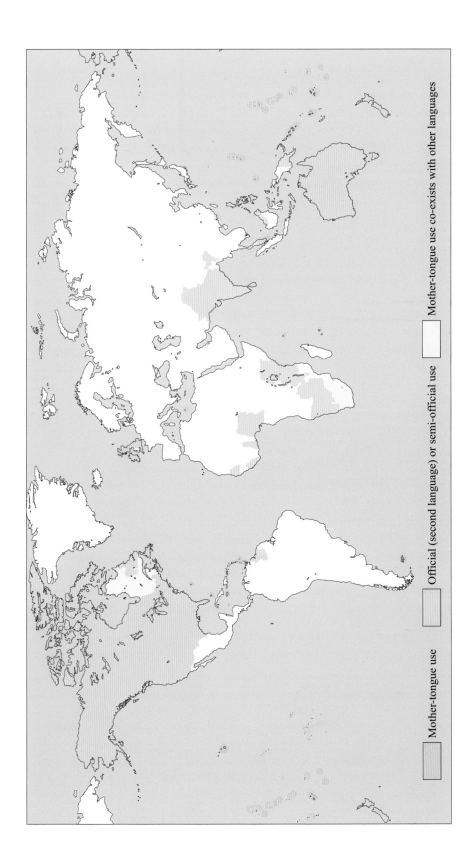

Figure 1.5 The spread of English across the globe, in terms of the territories where English is either a mother tongue or has some form of official status. In addition to the countries shown here, English is spoken as a foreign or international language in a great many more places around the world. (Adapted from Crystal, 1988, pp. 8–9.)

Mother-tongue use

Official (second language) or semi-official use

Mother-tongue use co-exists with other languages

spread is that there are now more users of English who are non-native speakers than those who speak it as their mother tongue. Some estimates suggest that almost 1,500 million people around the world speak English, and only 400 million of these are native speakers (Crystal, 2006, p. 424). In several countries people use English in addition to their native language or languages, and for many other people it is an international form of communication – that is, they use it specifically to talk to people with whom they do not share a mother tongue. In contexts such as these, the form of the language that is used is not necessarily identical to standard British or American English. It may well be something more akin to what Tan's mother speaks. In other words, non-standard forms such as those used by Tan's mother are widespread throughout the world, and in some contexts they are practically the norm. Yet as we can see from the reading, a common perception is that such forms are failed attempts to speak proper English, and are evaluated as being sub-standard.

Such evaluation does not only occur with respect to non-native English usage though. In the preface to his play *Pygmalion*, Shaw made the satirical assertion that 'it is impossible for an Englishman to open his mouth without making some other Englishman despise him' (1986 [1913], p. 327). He wrote this a century ago, and it might be thought that since then the UK has become less class-conscious and that prejudices based on someone's background are not as widespread as they once were. Up to a point this may well be true, but that is not to say that evaluation about people's way of speaking – and especially their accent and dialect – no longer occurs. In fact, we engage in some form of evaluation of how others speak all the time, even if it is just in terms of spotting a distinctiveness in their manner of speech and associating it with a particular group identity.

Tan writes towards the beginning of her essay about 'the forms of standard English that I had learned in school and through books'. And it is the idea of the standard that is often key to the way that people's use of English is evaluated. It is standard English that acts as a benchmark against which other usages are compared – and often judged.

The next reading is an extract from a book called *English with an Accent* by Rosina Lippi-Green. In this section of the book, Lippi-Green discusses some definitions of a standard language, and points to a number of problems in the way these definitions conceive of the concept. She is writing specifically about standard US English, and is concentrating mostly on pronunciation (and thus accent). But the issues she raises are the same for any other standard English (e.g. standard British English), and can also apply to dialect.

Activity

This activity should take you about 30–40 minutes.

1 Before we examine the concept of standard English a little further, take a couple of minutes to jot down a few notes about what the term suggests to you. Do you think that the concept of a standard language is important, and if so why? Where do you think the standard language comes from, and how is it maintained?

2 Now turn to Reading 1.2. As you read, think about the following questions:

According to the definitions Lippi-Green analyses, what or who provides the model for standard English?

— the educated

What does she mean when she says that standard English is determined by those who have authority?

Why does she liken standard English to certain 'mythical, imaginary constructs'?

— we all believe it / part of culture / doesn't mean its right

Discussion

The central argument Lippi-Green puts forward is that the type of English promoted by dictionaries as being the model for 'standard English' is a usage originally associated with one particular section of society. The dictionaries she looks at all state that the usage they are describing is that of 'educated' native speakers. But when we start examining what this means in practice, the issue becomes rather complicated. Who exactly counts as an 'educated' speaker? Does someone have to be educated to a particular level, or have gone to a particular school or college, or be part of a particular profession? Her conclusion is that there is no way in which a dictionary can be an *objective* description of standard pronunciation of the language. Instead, it is modelled on the usage patterns (the dialect and accent) of a particular social group. And the reason that this group rather than another gets to provide the model for standard English is because the group has a position of power and influence in society. It thus has the authority to impose its norms on society and to promote them as standard. For this reason she likens the concept of standard English to 'mythical, imaginary constructions' such as unicorns and King Arthur. Standard English is an idea that many people believe in, but if taken too literally it belies the variety and diversity of the way people actually use the language.

If the idea of a standard English is in some ways an idealisation, how then does it come about? Has the notion always existed? Or was there a time when people didn't view variety as problematic, and didn't see some types of usage as more 'correct' than others?

In Reading 1.3 the British linguist David Crystal writes about the history of standard English and how it developed in the British Isles. His focus in this passage is on the period of Middle English – that is, the form the language took between the Norman Conquest and the beginning of the Renaissance (i.e. in the period from about 1100 to 1500).

Activity

Now turn to Reading 1.3. As you read, note the different ways Crystal suggests that a standard can be established, and how it happened in the case of English. What role is played by authority in the emergence of a standard?

This activity should take you about 30–40 minutes.

Discussion

Many of the ways Crystal suggests that a standard language can be established relate directly to the execution of authority by powerful institutions. Governments can select which dialect will be used as a standard, and then promote this via dictionaries and grammar books. Or the standard can evolve based on an influential literary tradition – and in this way standard languages are related to the establishments of literary canons. In the case of English, though, standardisation came about without the direct intervention of a single powerful institution. It was a more 'organic' process, the result of the influence of the publishing industry, of literary writers and scholars, of scientific institutions, of influential political and public figures, all combining over the years to promote one variety of the language over others. It was, nevertheless, a historical process. In the fourteenth century there was no real concept of standard English at all. By the eighteenth century the notion as we know it today had become fully formed.

Viewed from this perspective, standard English can be seen as a 'historical construct' rather than a naturally occurring phenomenon – that is, there is nothing inevitable or inviolable about standard English. If the history of the UK had been different, the nature of standard British English would very likely be different as well. Now that it has become established in society, however, it acts as a **prestige variety**, and in many contexts is seen as the most appropriate form of the language to use. In other words, it does now exist, for good or for bad, as the benchmark against which judgements about what is 'right' and what is 'wrong' are regularly made.

— a social dialect or accent that has a high status in society

1.4   Drawing on different dialects and languages

In Reading 1.1, Tan wrote of the way that she shifted between two different styles of English when talking to different people. She says she was doing this almost without registering it, and it was only when her mother was in the audience for her talk at the university – that is, when two different domains of her life came together – that she became self-conscious about the different 'Englishes' that she was regularly speaking. In this particular example, Tan was drawing attention to the fact that she used different styles of speech for different contexts. In Chapter 2 we'll explore this idea in greater detail with reference to the way that different domains of life often require different types of language use. In the final section of this chapter, though, I want to look at a related issue: how people draw on different accents, dialects and languages as part of the communicative process, and how the use of 'mixed' styles indicates something about someone's personal and cultural history.

Throughout this chapter we have been discussing ways in which *how* a person says something can be as meaningful as *what* he or she says, and we have noted that this is often related to the fact that the form of language people use is closely tied to their identity. Identity, though, is a complex issue. People rarely, if ever, fit into easily definable boxes. Everyone's personal biography and family history is different, and this unique background will contribute to who they are as an individual. This background will also have an influence on they way they speak, so that their language will have traces of the various different elements that combine to produce their identities. And this is true not just for individual people, but for groups within society as well.

To explore this issue, let's look again at a short exchange from *The Island*, which you read in Book 1. The play is written in English, but uses occasional words from other languages.

You may wish briefly to look back at the notes to Book 1, Chapter 4, Reading 4.1, which include information about the words from other languages.

Activity

This activity should take you about 15 minutes.

Read through the dialogue below and note the words and phrases that are not in English. Why do you think that there are a number of foreign words in what is otherwise an English-language dialogue?

JOHN   You know what I'm saying?

WINSTON   *Ja.*

JOHN   What?

WINSTON   What 'What'?

JOHN   What am I saying?

WINSTON   *Haai*, Johnny, man! I'm tired now! Let a man …

JOHN   I'm saying Don't be Hard-Arsed! You! When Hodoshe opens that door tomorrow say, '*Ja, Baas*' the right way. I don't want to be back on that bloody beach tomorrow just because you feel like being difficult.

(Fugard, 1993, scene 1, p. 204)

– emphasis
– emotion
– stress

Discussion

In this short exchange three different languages are being used. The main one is, of course, English. But in addition there are a few words in both Afrikaans ('*Ja, Baas*') and Xhosa ('*haai*', '*hodoshe*').

– has special legal status in a country

South Africa is a decidedly multilingual society, and the country presently has eleven **official languages**. For this reason it isn't odd that the characters should use a mix of different languages. They are not, after all, *foreign* languages for the society as a whole. They are all part of the general linguistic make up of South Africa as a nation. But they are also languages that have different histories within the country, and thus have different associations for different sections of the population. Afrikaans is the language that developed from the Dutch spoken by the colonising powers in the seventeenth century. In this exchange, John switches into Afrikaans when discussing what Winston should say to the warder: '*Ja, Baas*' ('Yes, boss'). In the context in which it is used here, Afrikaans appears to be a language related to institutional power – the characters use it when interacting with the authority figure in the play – and this may be a reflection of the language's colonial heritage. Xhosa, on the other hand, is a Bantu language that was spoken in the region before the colonial period. It is also the language originally spoken by Nelson Mandela's family. In this section of dialogue the characters use it on two occasions. Winston cries out '*Haai*' (a general exclamation of surprise or alarm), and it is used for the nickname they have for the chief warder, 'Hodoshe' (meaning 'carrion fly'). So Xhosa appears to be used here for more personal meanings: for the expression of emotions, and for the private nicknames they have for the figure of authority.

An 'official language' is one that has a special legal status in a country, and is used in contexts such as administration and education. During apartheid, there were only two official languages: English and Afrikaans. In 1994, after the end of apartheid, the new constitution gave official status to eleven languages: English, Afrikaans and nine indigenous African languages.

What we can see from this example is that not only does the mixing of several languages reflect the multilingual nature of the society, but that the choice of which language to use when is related to the history of the society and to the identity of the people involved in the discussion. The switch from one language to another is not random. Instead, the language in which different expressions are made is significant because of the associations that that language has in that society and for those particular characters.

On DVD 2, Kay McCormick and Raj Mesthrie from the University of Cape Town and Li Wei from the University of London discuss the way that people use different languages in their everyday speech, and how and why they switch from one to another. This is called **code-switching** and is a common practice in multilingual societies.

Activity

Now listen to 'Code-switching' on DVD 2. Pay attention to what is said about how the linguistic environment of South Africa – and the fact that the country has so many official languages, all of which have different histories within society – influences the choices people make about the language they use, and how such choices relate to people's identities. You may also like to think back to the interviews with the three poets in Section 1.2 and how they talked about the creative possibilities of switching between different varieties and languages.

Code switching - alternating between languages during a conversation

Code mixing - alternating between languages within a sentence

Conclusion

Throughout this chapter we have looked at a number of different ways in which language use varies from person to person and from community to community. A key theme has been that this variation is linked to identity – that the way we use language relates to the way the community in which we live or from which we come uses language. And because of this, the simple act of speaking (irrespective of what we actually say) will indicate something about our social and regional background.

An important point to add though is that language variation is *dynamic*. As communities alter (as people move from place to place, as culture changes under the influence of the media or because of particular social or historical events), the language used by the community will also alter. Furthermore, people aren't locked in to using a particular dialect simply because that was the predominant speaking style of the place where they grew up. People can and do tailor their language to the situations in which they find themselves. As we saw with Amy Tan, people often shift between different language styles for different audiences. And as we heard from the poets Valerie Bloom, W.N. Herbert and Ian McMillan, people can draw creatively on the associations that different language varieties have and can actively use these associations as part of the communicative process. In the next chapter we'll further explore some of these ideas by looking at the way that language relates to the context in which it is used, and at how people exploit linguistic conventions for the purposes of expression.

References

Crystal, D. (1988) *The English Language*, Harmondsworth, Penguin.

Crystal, D. (2005) *The Stories of English*, London, Penguin.

Crystal, D. (2006) 'English worldwide' in Hogg, F. and Denison, D. (eds) *A History of the English Language*, Cambridge, Cambridge University Press.

Esling, J.H. (1998) 'Everyone has an accent except me' in Bauer, L. and Trudgill, P. (eds) *Language Myths*, London, Penguin.

Fugard, A. (1993) *The Township Plays* (ed. D. Walder), Oxford, Oxford University Press.

Harris, J. (1993) 'The grammar of Irish English' in Milroy, J. and Milroy, L. (eds) *Real English: The Grammar of English Dialects in the British Isles*, London, Longman.

Hickey, R. (2007) *Irish English: History and Present-Day Forms*, Cambridge, Cambridge University Press.

Lippi-Green, R. (1997) *English with an Accent*, London, Routledge.

Shaw, G.B. (1960 [1907]) *Major Barbara*, Harmondsworth, Penguin.

Shaw, G.B. (1986 [1913]) *The Portable Bernard Shaw* (ed. S. Weintraub), London, Penguin.

Smith, J.J. (1996) 'Ear-rhyme, eye-rhyme and traditional rhyme: English and Scots in Robert Burns's "Brigs of Ayr"', *The Glasgow Review*, vol. 4, pp. 74–85.

Stockwell, P. (2002) *Sociolinguistics: A Resource Book for Students*, Abingdon, Routledge.

Synge, J.M. (1981 [1905]) *J.M. Synge: The Complete Plays*, London, Methuen.

Tan, A. (1990) 'Mother tongue', *The Threepenny Review*, vol. 43, pp. 7–8.

Trudgill, P. (1999) *The Dialects of England*, Oxford, Blackwell.

Twain, M. (1989 [1897]) *Following the Equator: A Journey Around the World*, vol. 1, New York, Dover.

Twain, M. (1999 [1884]) *Huckleberry Finn*, Oxford, Oxford University Press.

Van Doren, C. (1919) 'Some play-party songs from Eastern Illinois', *Journal of American Folklore*, vol. 32, no. 126, pp. 486–96.

Watson, K. (2009) 'Regional variation in English accents and dialects' in Culpeper, J., Katamba, F., Kerswill, P., Wodak, R. and McEnery, T. (eds) *English Language: Description, Variation and Context*, Hounslow, Palgrave Macmillan.

Further reading

Crystal, D. (2005) *The Stories of English*, London, Penguin.

Bauer, L. and Trudgill, P. (eds) *Language Myths*, London, Penguin.

Stockwell, P. (2002) *Sociolinguistics: A Resource Book for Students*, Abingdon, Routledge.

Readings

Reading 1.1: Mother tongue

I am not a scholar of English or literature. I cannot give you much more than personal opinions on the English language and its variations in this country or others.

I am a writer. And by that definition, I am someone who has always loved language. I am fascinated by language in daily life. I spend a great deal of my time thinking about the power of language – the way it can evoke an emotion, a visual image, a complex idea, or a simple truth. Language is the tool of my trade. And I use them all – all the Englishes I grew up with.

Recently, I was made keenly aware of the different Englishes I do use. I was giving a talk to a large group of people, the same talk I had already given to half a dozen other groups. The nature of the talk was about my writing, my life, and my book, *The Joy Luck Club*. The talk was going along well enough, until I remembered one major difference that made the whole talk sound wrong. My mother was in the room. And it was perhaps the first time she had heard me give a lengthy speech – using the kind of English I have never used with her. I was saying things like, 'The intersection of memory upon imagination' and 'There is an aspect of my fiction that relates to thus-and-thus' – a speech filled with carefully wrought grammatical phrases, burdened, it suddenly seemed to me, with nominalized forms, past perfect tenses, conditional phrases – all the forms of standard English that I had learned in school and through books, the forms of English I did not use at home with my mother.

Just last week, I was walking down the street with my mother, and I again found myself conscious of the English I was using, the English I do use with her. We were talking about the price of new and used furniture and I heard myself saying this: 'Not waste money that way.' My husband was with us as well, and he didn't notice any switch in my English. And then I realized why. It's because over the twenty years we've been together I've often used that same kind of English with him, and sometimes he even uses it with me. It has become our language of intimacy, a different sort of English that relates to family talk, the language I grew up with.

So you'll have some idea of what this family talk I heard sounds like, I'll quote what my mother said during a recent conversation which I videotaped and then transcribed. During this conversation, my mother was talking about a political gangster in Shanghai who had the same last name as her family's, Du, and how the gangster in his early years wanted to be adopted by her family which was rich by comparison. Later, the gangster became more powerful, far richer than my mother's family, and one day showed up at my mother's wedding to pay his respects. Here's what she said in part:

> Du Yusong having business like fruit stand. Like off the street kind. He is Du like Du Zong – but not Tsung-ming Island people. The local people call putong, the river east side, he belong to that side local people. That man want to ask Du Zong father take him in like become own family. Du Zong father wasn't look down on him, but didn't take seriously, until that man big like become a mafia. Now important person, very hard to inviting him. Chinese way, came only to show respect, don't stay for dinner. Respect for making big celebration, he shows up. Mean gives lots of respect. Chinese custom. Chinese social life that way. If too important won't have to stay too long. He come to my wedding. I didn't see, I heard it. I gone to boy's side, they have YMCA dinner. Chinese age I was 19.

You should know that my mother's expressive command of English belies how much she actually understands. She reads the Forbes report, listens to Wall Street Week, converses daily with her stockbroker, reads all of Shirley MacLaine's books with ease – all kinds of things I can't begin to understand. Yet some of my friends tell me they understand fifty percent of what my mother says. Some say they understand eighty to ninety percent. Some say they understand none of it, as if she were speaking pure Chinese. But to me, my mother's English is perfectly clear, perfectly natural. It's my mother tongue. Her language, as I hear it, is vivid, direct, full of observation and imagery. That was the language that helped shape the way I saw things, expressed things, made sense of the world.

Lately, I've been giving more thought to the kind of English my mother speaks. Like others, I have described it to people as 'broken' or 'fractured' English. But I wince when I say that. It has always bothered me that I can think of no way to describe it other than 'broken,' as if it were damaged and needed to be fixed, as if it lacked a certain wholeness and soundness. I've heard other terms used, 'limited English,' for example. But they seem just as bad, as if everything is limited, including people's perception of the limited English speaker.

I know this for a fact, because when I was growing up, my mother's 'limited' English limited *my* perception of her. I was ashamed of her English. I believed that her English reflected the quality of what she had to say. That is, because she expressed them imperfectly her thoughts were imperfect. And I had plenty of empirical evidence to support me: the fact that people in department stores, at banks, and at restaurants did not take her seriously, did not give her good service, pretended not to understand her, or even acted as if they did not hear her.

My mother has long realized the limitations of her English as well. When I was fifteen, she used to have me call people on the phone to pretend I was she. In this guise, I was forced to ask for information or even to complain and yell at people who had been rude to her. One time it was a call to her stockbroker in New York. She had cashed out her small portfolio and it just so happened we were going to go to New York the next week, our very first trip outside California. I had to get on the phone and say in an adolescent voice that was not very convincing, 'This is Mrs. Tan.'

And my mother was standing in the back whispering loudly, 'Why he don't send me check, already two weeks late. So mad he lie to me, losing me money.'

And then I said in perfect English, 'Yes, I'm getting rather concerned. You had agreed to send the check two weeks ago, but it hasn't arrived.'

Then she began to talk more loudly, 'What he want, I come to New York tell him front of his boss, you cheating me?' And I was trying to calm her down, make her be quiet, while telling the stockbroker, 'I can't tolerate any more excuses. If I don't receive the check immediately, I am going to have to speak to your manager when I'm in New York next week.' And sure enough, the following week there we were in front of this astonished stockbroker, and I was sitting there red-faced and quiet, and my mother, the real Mrs. Tan, was shouting at his boss in her impeccable broken English.

Source: Tan, A. (1990) 'Mother tongue', *The Threepenny Review*, vol. 43, pp. 7–8.

Reading 1.2: What we call Standard US English

People are quite comfortable with the idea of a standard language, so much so that they have no trouble describing and defining it, much in the same way that most people could draw a unicorn, or describe a being from *Star Trek*'s planet Vulcan, or tell us who King Arthur was and why he needed a Round Table. For the most part these definitions will be firmly founded in the understanding that these are mythical, imaginary constructions; nevertheless, the definitions will have much in common, because they are part of our shared cultural heritage.

The way we conceive and define Standard US English brings to light a number of assumptions and misassumptions about language. *Merriam-Webster's Collegiate Dictionary* (tenth edition, 1993), which proclaims itself *The Voice of Authority*, provides a typical definition:

> Standard English: the English that with respect to spelling, grammar, pronunciation, and vocabulary is substantially uniform though not devoid of regional differences, that is well established by usage in the formal and informal speech and writing of the educated, and that is widely recognized as acceptable wherever English is spoken and understood.

This definition assumes that the written and spoken language are equal, in terms of both how they are used, and how they should be used. It sets spelling and pronunciation on a common footing, and compounds this generalization by bringing in both formal and informal language use. While the definition makes some room for 'regional differences' it makes none at all for social ones, and in fact it is quite definite about the social construction of Standard US English: it is the language of the educated. What is meant by 'educated' is left unstated in this entry, and its implications are not fully explored anywhere else in the dictionary. What language might be spoken by those who are the *opposite* of the educated is also not made clear, but whoever these people are, they are drawn into the definition by its final component: Standard US English is *acceptable wherever English is spoken and understood*. The lexicographer assumes the consent of the non-educated, uneducated, or lesser educated to the authority of the educated in matters of written and spoken language.

Other definitions bring some important generalizations about Standard US English to the fore: *Cambridge International Dictionary of English* (first edition, 1995) also cites educated speakers as the sole possessors of the standard language, but they bring in a specific subgroup of the educated in that they assert that 'most announcers on the BBC speak standard English.' *Chambers Dictionary* (1994) is more specific about the path to Standard US English: 'the form of English taught in schools.' In 1978 the *English Journal* noted a general perception in the public of a '"standard standard". Some people call it "broadcast" or "publications" standard, because most newspapers and television news shows use it.'

More specific information on exactly how the lexicographer draws on the language of the educated is provided by interviews with the pronunciation editor at Merriam-Webster which appeared in various newspapers around the appearance of that dictionary's tenth edition. It falls to the pronunciation editor to decide which possible pronunciations are included in the dictionary, and how they are ordered. 'Usage dictates acceptability,' he is reported as saying. 'There is no other non-arbitrary way to decide' (*New York Times*, July 22, 1993: C1, C8).

In order to pin down this 'majority rule' the editor listens to 'talk shows, medical shows, interviews, news, commentary, the weather' (ibid.) on the radio and on television. The editorial preface to the dictionary is more specific about this procedure; it lists politicians, professors, curators, artists, musicians, doctors, engineers, preachers, activists, and journalists among the type of educated person whose English is consulted as a part of this process.

> In truth, though, there can be no objective standard for correct pronunciation other than the usage of thoughtful and, in particular, educated speakers of English. Among such speakers one hears much variation in pronunciation … [our attempt is to] include all variants of a word that are used by educated speakers.
>
> (*Merriam-Webster's Collegiate Dictionary*, tenth edition, 1993: 31a)

The editors claim an objective standard (that of the language of the educated) and at the same time they acknowledge variation among educated speakers. This apparent inconsistency is resolved by the policy which includes *all variants that are used by educated speakers*. A close look at the pronunciations listed in the dictionary, however, indicates that this cannot be the case. An entry with three or more possible pronunciations is rare. If Merriam-Webster's *Dictionary* truly intends to include all pronunciations of the educated, then their definition of who is educated must be very narrow.

It must be clear that this process cannot be representative in any real way. What proportion of even the *educated* population has regular access to the broadcast media? How many of us discuss our views on the budget, on foreign affairs, or on local government in a forum which is broadcast to a wider audience? The *uneducated*, who by the dictionary definition must constitute the greatest number of native speakers of English, are even less represented.

Perhaps there is no way to write a dictionary which is truly descriptive in terms of pronunciation; perhaps it is necessary to choose one social group to serve as a model. Perhaps there is even some rationale for using the 'educated' as this group. But there is nothing *objective* about this practice. It is the ordering of social groups in terms of who has authority to determine how language is *best used*.

Source: Lippi-Green, R. (1997) *English with an Accent*, London, Routledge, pp. 53–5.

Reading 1.3: The emerging standard

Standard languages arise in many ways. They can evolve over a long period of time associated with a particular body of religious or literary writing. Or an official body can be created (an Academy) which 'institutionalizes' a language by organizing the compilation of dictionaries, grammars, and manuals of style. In a further scenario, a standard can arrive, quite literally, overnight: a government selects a dialect of a language, prepares its people, and on a certain legally defined day it becomes the medium of national communication. Sometimes, more than one dialect is selected as the basis of the standard, and a planned amalgamation of forms takes place, as happened to Romansh in Switzerland in the 1980s when Rumantsch Grischun was devised, based on a collation of forms from the major dialects. It is even possible for a country to have two standard varieties of a language, as in the case of Norway, where Bokmål and Nynorsk have been in official coexistence since 1884.

In England, at the end of the Middle Ages, a standard language began to emerge, but it was in no way planned or institutionalized. There was no government intervention. No official bodies were established – the age predated the arrival of Academies in Europe (the first such body, in Italy, was not established until 1582). There were no pundits arguing for a policy of standardization. There was not even a long-standing body of comprehensible English classical literature to look back to: Old English was a foreign language to most people by then, as William Caxton observed in his Preface to *Eneydos* (*c*.1490):

> And also my lorde Abbot of Westmynster ded [did] do shewe to me late certayn evydences wryton in olde Englysshe for to reduce it into our Engylysshe now usid. And certaynly it was wreton in suche wyse that it was more lyke to Dutche than Englysshe: I coude not reduce ne [nor] brynge it to be understonden.

In 1400 Chaucer's writing had yet to achieve classical status, and English translation of the Bible had hardly begun, notwithstanding Wycliffe's pioneering role in the 1380s. At the beginning of the fifteenth century, anyone who might have reflected on the need for a standard English language would have found it difficult to see where it could possibly come from. Yet, by the end of the century, its basis was definitely there.

It is difficult to resist the conclusion that Standard English, like Harriet Beecher Stowe's Topsy, 'just growed' – largely unselfconsciously during the fifteenth century, and increasingly self-aware thereafter. The growth took a long time – some 300 years, indeed, before the phenomenon, as we recognize it today, was firmly established. It is important to reiterate: only the *basis* of Standard English existed by 1500. Comparing the kind of language which was being written and spoken in those days to the kind of language we associate with Standard English now, we see a wide range of differences. The clear-cut distinction between 'correct' and 'incorrect' did not exist in late Middle English – that was an eighteenth-century development. There was much greater flexibility over the range of forms which educated people were able to use. And a great deal of variation, a legacy of earlier Middle English, was still in evidence. Apart from anything else, the language was still experiencing the consequences of the period of radical grammatical change which had begun at the end of the Old English period. In the fifteenth century it was undergoing a major shift in pronunciation norms. And its lexicon was continuing to grow rapidly through the introduction of large numbers of loanwords. A standard language presupposes a certain amount of stability: people have to be using the same set of rules, enabling them to distinguish between what is 'right' and what is 'wrong'. It would take a while before these judgements would be made with the kind of arrogant confidence which later became routine.

Source: Crystal, D. (2005) *The Stories of English*, London, Penguin, pp. 222–3.

2 Writing and register

Philip Seargeant

Contents

Aims

This chapter will:

- introduce you to the ways in which writing differs from speech, and to the fact that the way a text is structured is a vital element in the communicative process
- examine how language differs depending on the purpose for which it is being used
- look at the ways texts create different perspectives on events through the manipulation of their structure.

Materials you will need

- DVD 2 (audio)

Introduction: language as a tool

In the last chapter we looked at the ways in which language is determined by its users, and at how the phenomenon of dialect plays an important role in people's identities. We examined how differences in language use occur from social group to social group (i.e. different groups have different dialects), and we observed that all language use is to some extent systematic and follows set patterns of use. In this chapter we move on to the subject of language that is determined by the uses to which it is put rather than by the geographical or social background of the people who use it. As was mentioned in Chapter 4 of Book 1, this type of language is called a **register**, and is another fundamental aspect of everyday communication. Register is another way in which *how* something is said or written can be as important for the meaning of the message as *what* is said or written.

eg academic register

Let's begin by considering the metaphor of language being a tool. Like a tool, language is used for getting things done. We use language to ask for things, to explain things, to give instructions, to apologise, to make people laugh, and so on.

Activity

Take a few minutes to make a list of what you have used language to do so far today. How many different tasks have you achieved by means of language? Would you have been able to achieve these without recourse to speaking or writing?

Discussion

So far today I've done a variety of things using language. These range from greeting members of my family, to holding meetings with colleagues, to marking students' assignments. I've spoken to a colleague in Leeds on the phone to make an appointment to meet; I've emailed a professor in Germany inviting him to contribute to one of our courses; and at lunchtime I used language to order a sandwich. Plus, of course, I've been sitting in front of the computer writing this chapter, trying to craft something that will act as an educational tool for this module. In fact, I'd say that the majority of my day so far has involved using language. I've used both spoken and written forms of language, some instances of which have taken a lot of effort to produce (the email to the professor in Germany; the drafting of this chapter), and some of which I've done practically without thinking about at all (the greetings, the ordering of lunch). In each case, I've had a particular objective I've been trying to fulfil. And without having recourse to language – and to the various forms of communication technology which act as a medium for my use of language (pen and paper, telephone, computer, etc.) – I'd have been able to achieve virtually none of these things.

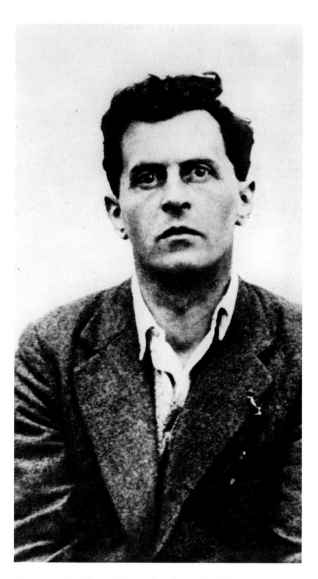

Figure 2.1   The philosopher Ludwig Wittgenstein. Private collection. Unknown photographer. Photo: © The Bridgeman Art Library.

The metaphor of language being a tool was notably used by the philosopher Ludwig Wittgenstein (1889–1951; Figure 2.1) in the middle of the twentieth century. In describing language in this way, Wittgenstein shifted the study of language away from the abstract analysis of its structure to the way it is actually used – and especially to the question of what it is used for. Prior to this, most mainstream linguistics had concentrated on describing the various components of a language and how these parts fitted together. Linguists spent the majority of their time cataloguing and analysing the grammatical workings of different languages, and generalising rules about this structure. Wittgenstein's writings – particularly his book *Philosophical Investigations* (1953) – were instrumental in shifting the focus of attention to what language is used to achieve.

In proposing this view of language, he writes: 'Think of the tools in a tool-box: there is a hammer, pliers, a saw, a screw-driver, a rule, a glue-pot, glue, nails and screws. – The functions of words are as diverse as the functions of these objects' (Wittgenstein, 1953, para. 11). A corollary to this view of language is that, if we want to get something done, we need to use the *correct* tool. For example, we can't successfully bang a nail into a wall with a screwdriver. Or, at least, we could, but it wouldn't be the most efficient way to achieve the objective, and could easily end with us damaging ourselves or ruining the job. The same applies to the use of language. We need to use the right type of language for the right type of activity. And what counts as the right type of tool will depend on the task at hand and the circumstances in which it is to be used.

Take, for example, the task of writing an essay. When you are writing your assignments for this or for other modules, you need to ensure that you use the correct tone of language, that you employ the right vocabulary (including the use of any specialised terminology), and that you follow the appropriate structuring and formatting conventions (i.e. that you include an introduction and conclusion, you have a central argument, you reference any works you may quote, etc.). All these are elements of an **academic register**, and they are part of the toolkit you use to express yourself in an academic environment. It would be inappropriate, for example, to write an academic essay using the same type of language that you use for writing a text-message to a friend. Not only would it give the wrong impression to your tutor, but the type of language would not allow you to discuss the complex concepts and issues that are involved in academic study. In effect, using the wrong type of language would not get the job done properly.

In this chapter we'll look at what comprises a register, and at how people use different registers in their everyday lives. In doing this, we'll concentrate, for the most part, on examples of written language. We'll examine how different activities determine the type of language used for that activity, and at how written texts frame our expectations about their meaning from the way they conventionally organise information. Language defined by its use is, of course, also a feature of spoken discourse, and the chapter will also discuss a few examples of spoken interaction drawn both from real-life settings and from literature and drama. In fact we'll begin by looking at the differences between spoken and written language. As you will see, the distinction between spoken and written language is also in part a result of the different purposes to which these two ways of using language are put. In other words, speech and writing are different tools that we use for different types of task.

2.1   Differences between speech and writing

If you were asked what the difference is between speech and writing you might well reply that the answer is startlingly obvious: one involves making a variety of sounds with your voice, while the other involves making marks on a piece of paper or on a screen. They both use identical forms of language, you may say; the difference between them is just a matter of the means by which that language is actually transmitted. To an extent such an answer is perfectly correct. In modern British society – and in many other societies – a large proportion of the population mostly use the same language, i.e. English, when speaking and writing. But as we saw in the previous chapter, within the broad category of 'English' there can be great variety in the way people actually use the language, and this variety is systematic (i.e. it has a regularity to it, and is not random or arbitrary) and related to the social environments in which people live. One question we could ask, therefore, is whether similar variety exists between the spoken and the written **modes** of language use. Are speaking and writing identical in all ways except for the fact that one uses the voice and the other the alphabet? Or is there something fundamentally different not only in the mode of expression but also in the form of the language they require?

The answer to this partly lies in the nature of the mode used to transmit the message. As I mentioned above, whenever we use language we do so in combination with another sort of tool, such as a computer, a phone, a pen or simply our own voice. If I want to write a letter, I need pen and paper, plus a system that will ensure that my letter is delivered to the person to which it is addressed. And it is usually the case that the type of language we use in any given situation will be influenced by the type of tool we use. This influence can be seen not only in the obvious superficial differences between speaking and writing (the former involves modulations of sound in the atmosphere; the latter involves marks on a page or screen), but also in the way that the communicative message is structured.

When writing a letter, for example, I have to take into account the fact that the person to whom I am writing is not physically present and so cannot respond or ask for clarification about any points. I also have to take into account that the recipient will not read the letter for a day or two, so I need to be explicit about things like time and place. All these

The word 'mode' refers to the means by which a message is communicated. Different modes include speaking, writing, or – in the case of sign language – gesture.

points will affect the way I compose the message, with the result that, even if the general content of the message is much the same as it would have been if I'd been able to talk directly to the person, the actual shape of the message will be very different. In other words, speech and writing are likely to have different structures because they are used for different communicative purposes, and because they allow for different communicative possibilities.

Activity

Look at the two short pieces of discourse below, both extracts from Gee (2005, pp. 128 and 127–8 respectively). Which of them do you think was originally spoken, and which was written? What features of the language led you to decide which category to put them in?

Example 1   — *written*

> Connected speech is like a set of boxes within boxes. The focuses of consciousness (lines), most of which are single clauses, are grouped together as one large, unitary body of information, like the setting of a story. This larger body of information is itself composed of stanzas, each of which takes a single perspective on an event, state of affairs, or character.

— formal / descriptive / comprehensive

Example 2

> last yesterday
> when my father
> in the morning
> an' he …
> there was a hook
> on the top of the stairway
> an' my father was pickin me up
> an' I got stuck on the hook
> up there
>
> an' I hadn't had breakfast
> he wouldn't take me down
> until I finished all my breakfast
> cause I didn't like oatmeal either

— sounds / phonetic / expressionist

Discussion

Example 1 is a piece of written discourse. It is from an academic book – one about Language Studies, as it happens. Example 2 is a transcript of a piece of spoken discourse. It is an extract from a short narrative by a seven-year-old girl from the USA. There are a number of differences between the two extracts. The first concerns the way that they are laid out on the page. Example 1 is set out in a way that is conventional for written texts. Each sentence follows directly after the previous one, and they are separated by full stops. Each new sentence begins with a capital letter, and the different phrases within it are marked off by commas. Example 2, on the other hand, doesn't follow these conventions. There is no use of formal punctuation rules; instead phrases (or rather, short chunks of meaning) are distinguished by a line break.

There is also a difference in the type of vocabulary used, and in how the words are strung together. Example 1 is more complex in this respect. It uses standard spelling, along with phrases such as 'unitary body of information', and it nests clauses inside one another to allow for a level of precision in the meaning it is expressing (e.g. 'The focuses of consciousness (lines), most of which are single clauses, are grouped together'). Example 2 uses a far less intricate structure of clauses. The structure basically involves one small chunk of the story following directly on from another. We can almost see the path of the meaning unfolding before us, as the speaker wends forward with the narrative, occasionally making wrong turns and needing to correct herself. The result is a burst of short, repetitive phrases, some of which are ungrammatical, and some of which simply get abandoned halfway through.

Part of the reason why Example 2 is less complicated is because the speaker is a young child. But it is also because spoken language relies much more on the capabilities of our memory, whereas written language allows for a more considered approach to the composition. In writing we can take time picking out the right word, and ensuring that all the grammatical elements of the sentence agree with one another and that the meaning flows in a smooth and coherent way. In other words, in written discourse we can *edit* our utterances in a way which simply isn't possible in spoken discourse.

Transcripts

As was noted at the beginning of the previous chapter, all the 'spoken' language in this book has been written down. In other words, Example 2 in the previous activity is a **transcript** of actual speech. That is, it is a *representation* of speech, in much the same way that the extracts from the novels and plays in Chapter 1 were. But whereas the extracts from literature were invented approximations of how people speak (i.e. they were fabricated examples of language use), this transcript is a record of a real instance of speech. We can mark this distinction by saying that the literary examples – especially the extracts from the two plays – were **scripts**, whereas this real-life example is a transcript. The intention of a transcript is to document as accurately as possible what was said, in such a way that the person reading it can get a clear impression of what was going on. For this reason, things like pauses, overlaps or misspoken words are often included. In Chapter 3, we'll look at how, when creative writers come to represent 'authentic' speech, they often ignore these features, and create something (a script) that gives the impression of being naturalistic, but in fact is not.

2.2 Register: language defined by its use

Comparing examples of spoken and written discourse shows us that the structure of language can be influenced by the way it is used. The basic difference between spoken and written language is simply that one uses the voice and the other the pen or computer. It is no more complicated than that. But the *implications* of these different modes – that communication using the voice is likely to be more immediate, more reliant on the context in which it occurs and on the human capabilities of the speakers, and that communication using pen or computer often allows for more deliberation and is more permanent – result in a range of marked differences in the structure of the language.

In what other ways, then, does language differ according to the uses to which it is put? The simple answer is: in a great variety of ways. Much as there is huge diversity in the dialects of English, so also there is great diversity in the different registers of the language. And just as the diversity and variety of dialects complicates simplistic ideas about what English is, so the same thing applies to the concept of different registers. For example, it may be that, although you consider yourself to be a highly proficient English speaker, there will be certain situations where you will struggle to understand what people are talking about simply because you are not used to the register of language they are using. The Russian literary critic Mikhail Bakhtin (1895–1975; Figure 2.2) writes that:

> Many people who have an excellent command of a language often feel quite helpless in certain spheres of communication precisely because they do not have a practical command of the generic forms used in the given spheres. Frequently a person who has an excellent command of speech in some areas of cultural communication, who is able to read a scholarly paper or engage in a scholarly discussion, who speaks very well on social questions, is silent or very awkward in social conversation.

> (Bakhtin, 1986, p. 78)

Bakhtin is here suggesting that different types of communicative encounter (different 'generic forms' of communication) have different rules and conventions, and that one needs to know these in order to operate successfully in particular situations. You may have experienced something similar yourself. Whereas you might be perfectly competent in certain areas of social life when it comes to communicating in English, in other areas you might find yourself suddenly less confident and feel that your language is 'letting you down'. For example, you may feel entirely comfortable talking in great detail about a sport or hobby, but when speaking to a mortgage advisor you may find yourself struggling to understand vital terms or feeling self-conscious about the style of language you are using. Or perhaps in your case it is the opposite, and you can talk happily about financial issues but struggle if the conversation turns to football.

Figure 2.2   Mikhail Bakhtin, Russian literary theorist and philosopher.

Activity

Look at the following two extracts, both of which are from written commentaries of sports matches. Both these texts were published by major news networks and both are in contemporary English. To what extent can you understand them? Are there any words you don't understand – either because they appear completely new to you, or because they seem to be used in an unfamiliar way?

This activity should take you about 20 minutes.

Extract 1

The Dodgers made it 3–1 in the bottom of the third when Ethier was hit by a pitch, moved up on a walk to Ramirez and took third on James Loney's flyout.

Third baseman Mark DeRosa made a diving, backhanded stop of Blake's infield hit down the line, but his throw to second sailed into right field. In the second, DeRosa banged his right hand into Loney while scrambling back to first base on a lineout.

Wolf let St. Louis load the bases with no outs in the first. But he allowed just one run on Ryan Ludwick's bloop single to center between Kemp and Ronnie Belliard, and then Kemp put Los Angeles ahead.

(Harris, 2009)

Extract 2

1158: Aus 356–6. Fred will have one more, at least. That's nightmarish to face – pinging up from short of a length and crashing in to Johnson's bat handle – but that's well played, pulled off his nose for two to deep midwicket. 166 needed by Australia, and Johnson is settling in a little – 26 not out, hogging the strike from his more experienced pardner.

1204: Aus 356–7. Drift and dip did for Clarkie there – Swann gave it some air, Pup got monkeyed in the flight and the ball then turned just enough from outside off to thunk the top of the off peg. As bowling changes go, that's useful …

1229: He's starting to look a little weary now, Fred – Siddle jabs down on two in-dippers and gets the second down to long leg for a single. Johnson defends one away, takes a single off the fifth and exposes Siddle to what could be Flintoff's last ball. In-swinging yorker dug out – no-ball, so he'll have another pop. He turns off a run-up of about 10 paces – BOWLED HIM!

(Fordyce, 2009)

Discussion

Extract 1 is a report from the Associated Press on a baseball game from the USA; Extract 2 is part of an online commentary from the BBC about a cricket match: the second Test in the Ashes series at Lord's in 2009. If you're familiar with these sports and their rules, you'll probably have understood the passages easily enough. If you don't know much about the sports, they probably didn't make much sense to you.

Extract 1 is full of specialist terminology. The first sentence, for example, includes the following terms: 'The Dodgers made it 3–1 in *the bottom of the third* when Ethier was *hit by a pitch*, *moved up on a walk* to Ramirez and *took third* on James Loney's *flyout*.' In addition, you'd need to know to whom the proper names refer (the Dodgers, Ethier, James Loney), and what the significance of a 3–1 score is. If all the information that requires this specialist understanding were to be removed, we would be left with practically nothing that is meaningful. So although the passage is in English, and it uses fairly simple words such as 'third' and 'walk', the way it uses these words constitutes a specialist register, and can seem baffling if you aren't familiar with that register. (If you are familiar with baseball, and were able to understand the sentence easily enough, try finding someone who doesn't know anything about the sport and see how they fare with the sentence.)

Extract 2 is similar. Again, there is a lot of specialist terminology, such as 'short of a length', 'long-leg' and 'in-swinging yorker'. In addition, the writer assumes a great deal of shared knowledge with his readership. So, for example, players are referred to by nicknames (Fred, Clarkie), and the style of the language is very colloquial and full of slang terms that refer to specific elements of the game (e.g. 'Pup got monkeyed in the flight'). There is also a sense in this passage that the writer is playing with language – for example in using a spelling such as 'pardner' instead of 'partner' – which also conveys a sense of familiarity with the readership. So again, to understand this passage you need a knowledge of the technical vocabulary of cricket (e.g. Figure 2.3), a knowledge of the way players are referred to among this community of fans and a knowledge of the type of slang that is being used. If you are familiar with the context in either case, the texts will be easy to follow. But if you aren't, they could well appear almost nonsensical, despite the fact that they are both written in English.

Both the above examples are instances of specialised uses of language associated with particular activities. As such, both texts are addressed to particular groups of people: baseball fans and cricket fans respectively. We could say, therefore, that they are addressed to two particular

Figure 2.3   Specialist cricketing terms: *Silly Mid-Off* by Tony Husband. ©
Tony Husband.

communities of people, each of which share an interest in the respective
sports and, in pursuing this interest, have come to share a particular
way of talking about these sports. In other words, they are both
communities that use a particular register of language as a result of
their shared interest in a particular activity. In Language Studies, such a
group is known as a **discourse community**.

The linguist John Swales lists the following elements as being central to
the idea of a discourse community (1990, pp. 24–7):

- the existence of a shared set of goals
- the use of an established mechanism of communication between
members

- the use of a specialist vocabulary, and of particular genres of communication

- the existence of a core set of members who have an expertise in this use of language.

We'll look in more detail at the concept of 'genres' a little later in the chapter.

Communities of this sort may not interact face to face, or be located in a single geographical area. But their shared interest in a particular subject or activity means that their distinctive use of language still constitutes an important aspect of their behaviour, and as such is part of their identity.

Activity

Reading 2.1 is an example that Swales gives of a discourse community to which he himself belongs. Read the passage, and as you do so, think about the role language plays in the way the members of the community relate to each other. Does this community adhere to the other conditions that Swales has identified as being defining elements of a discourse community?

This activity should take you about 30 minutes.

Discussion

Swales states that this group meets all the criteria for a discourse community as he has outlined them. As we can see from the examples from the newsletter, the community uses a specialised register, full of technical terminology ('PPC' and 'CIP'), which is mostly incomprehensible to the outsider. (It's worth noting that discourse communities don't necessarily need to have *such* specialised interests.) The group is geographically dispersed across the globe, and the members rarely if ever meet face to face, but instead communicate by means of the journal and newsletter. There is a core of expert members, and new members wishing to participate need to adapt their own linguistic practices to the community's norms (which was something Swales himself had to do, and found rather challenging at first). And of course, they have a common goal, which acts as the *raison d'être* for the community.

The next activity invites you to think about your own discourse communities.

Activity

Try to identify any discourse communities of which you are a member. It may be related to your work, to a hobby, or to an organisation of which you are a member. What specialist language is used in this community, and what purposes does this type of language fulfil? Do members experience any particular challenges when they first join the community?

Discussion

One example of a discourse community of which you are a member is that of Open University students. When people first study with The Open University they often find the amount of jargon and specialist vocabulary overwhelming. They suddenly find themselves forced to contend with things such as eTMAs, the VLE and countless other specialist terms. Lots of these are shorthand ways of referring to particular elements of the learning and teaching process, so they are useful once you have learned them. In other words they have a particular function, and are examples of language being used in an efficient and precise way for the purposes of achieving a specific task. But for an outsider they sound obscure and probably completely meaningless.

In the next activity you will listen to people from two different professions – chefs and beekeepers – discuss the specialist use of language they have to deal with as part of their work, and talk about some of the challenges they experienced when first joining these discourse communities.

This activity should take you about 30–40 minutes.

Activity

Now listen to 'Discourse communities' on DVD 2, which includes two further examples of groups who use a specialist language as part their occupation. While listening, think about how similar their experiences are to the answers you gave in the activity above.

As we have seen, one of the key functions of a specialist register is to allow people to communicate with a high level of precision. Specialist terms, such as those used by stamp collectors or Open University students and staff, allow for the discussion of phenomena that non-specialists would not be concerned with. But as was also touched upon above, registers are not only used for the transmission of factual information. They can also express what is known as 'interpersonal meaning'. That is, they can be a means of communicating something about the identity of the speaker or writer. For example, the use by a doctor of a specialist register can be a way of indicating his or her professional identity. The ability to use a phrase such as 'tibial shaft fracture' rather than 'broken leg' points to membership of the medical community. In this way, register is a type of identity marker in much the same way that dialect is. But whereas dialect is related to geographical or social background, register is related to occupation or specialism, and to the part of people's identity that concerns what they do rather than where they are from.

The next activity contains examples of text that has appeared in the guidance notes, or 'small print', of various commercial services. They have been collected together by the Plain English Campaign, a society that, in its own words, campaigns 'against gobbledygook, jargon and misleading public information' (Plain English Campaign, 2010). They are all examples of what the Plain English Campaign considers to be unnecessarily complicated uses of English.

Activity

Read Examples 1–3, then try to 'translate' them into 'plain' English. Is anything lost in the translation? Why might these statements have been written in the way that they are?

This activity should take you about 20 minutes.

Example 1

If there are any points on which you require explanation or further particulars we shall be glad to furnish such additional details as may be required by telephone.

– pompous

If you have any questions, ask and we'll call you.

Example 2

It is important that you shall read the notes, advice and information detailed opposite then complete the form overleaf (all sections) prior to its immediate return to the Council by way of the envelope provided.

– authority

read & return.

Example 3

This Agreement and the benefits and advantages herein contained are personal to the Member and shall not be sold, assigned or transferred by the Member.

– legalistic

for the member only

Discussion

The Plain English Campaign supplies the following 'translations' for these three extracts:

Example 1

If you have any questions, please phone.

Example 2

Please read the notes opposite before you fill in the form. Then send it back to us as soon as possible in the envelope provided.

Example 3

Membership is not transferable.

Their versions are certainly much clearer than the originals, and manage to avoid any unnecessary words or phrases. But is anything lost by simplifying these statements like this? It probably depends on what we think the purpose of the statements is. One element of their purpose is to communicate basic factual information. But they are probably also intended to convey a certain impression to their readership. And the use of this rather complex (and perhaps pompous) register helps to do this. In other words, using phrases such as 'we shall be glad to furnish such additional details as may be required' is probably intended to lend a certain gravitas to the expression.

2.3   Communicative genres

So far we have looked at how choices about vocabulary and grammatical structure are used in the production of meaning. Another important aspect of meaning is the way a piece of discourse is organised at a more general level. To describe this aspect of the organisation of a text, we use the term **genre**. This term has been mentioned a number of times in the module so far. In Chapter 2 of Book 1, for example, it was used in the context of both Literature and Music, where it refers to different categories or types of work, such as, in the case of Literature: tragedy, sonnet or short story; and, in the case of Music: symphony, concerto or opera. The same general meaning applies in Language Studies, but here the term refers to *any* type of communicative act. It can refer to both a written text and to forms of spoken interaction. So, for example, in Language Studies a letter is referred to as a particular type of genre, as is an academic essay, an everyday conversation or a political speech. In each case, there are conventional patterns in the way the communicative act is organised. And because of these conventions, we already have a general framework in which to interpret the meaning of a communicative act simply by recognising the genre it is in.

Take, for example, the way you read a letter. Before you get to the first sentence you already know, based simply on the way it looks, that it is a letter – and indeed, you probably know what sort of letter it is. And because you know this, you can probably make rough inferences about what the content is going to be. If it is on headed paper, for example, and laid out with an address printed in the top corner, it is more likely to be a business letter than a personal note from a friend. So, as we can see, the genre creates certain expectations about the communication, and is a means of framing the content inside.

Activity

Now turn to Reading 2.2, which is an extract from an essay by Mikhail Bakhtin. We looked at a short passage from this reading in Section 2.2. Here you have a chance to read it again within the context of his argument that all communicative language use is framed in genres. While reading, think about how his argument ties in with our discussion above about how a letter is a type of communicative genre. Can you think of further common genres of communication?

This activity should take you about 30 minutes.

Discussion

Bakhtin's argument is that *all* our communicative encounters are structured by means of conventional genres of interaction. And yet, he contends, we take these genres completely for granted and so most of the time we don't even notice them. But the way we approach an encounter or communicative act, and the expectations we have about it, are informed by the conventions associated with it.

One good example of a genre of communicative interaction is the job interview. Most job interviews have a standard formula and include a number of specific elements. These range from expectations about how the participants should dress, about how the room is set out and where everyone sits, to expectations about how the conversation itself is organised. On a very basic level, the interviewer directs the proceedings, asks questions, takes notes and, at the end, allows the interviewee to put any questions he or she may have. Throughout the proceedings the language used is polite and mostly formal. All this is taken for granted – it is not explicitly explained when you step into the room for an interview. And if the candidate wants to get the job, he or she has to conform to the genre of the interaction and to know and negotiate these hidden conventions.

In the next activity you will read an extract from an article by Celia Roberts about the structure of job interviews in the UK. It begins with a transcript of part of an interview, which is followed by Roberts's analysis of how the interaction is structured. The candidate in the example is called Ire. He is from Nigeria, and is being interviewed for a low-paid delivery job. Roberts describes the eventual outcome of his interview as 'Borderline successful'. The analysis she provides is rather complex, so you may need to read the extract more than once. I'll go over the key points she raises in the activity discussion. Roberts suggests that the interview is structured around implicit norms. As you read, think about what the implications of this are for Ire and for the type of responses he gives. The details of this particular communicative genre are more subtle than the very basic formula I outlined above. Roberts writes of the way that British job interviews today are often structured around a 'competency framework' – that is, there are a number of key concepts such as team-working, self-management, good time-keeping, customer focus, etc., that are considered to be important attributes for a good employee. The interviewer will thus ask questions around these concepts, and is looking to see how well the candidate picks up on these.

Activity

Now turn to Reading 2.3. To what extent does Ire manage to pick up on the key concepts that make up a competency framework and present himself as aware of and able to fulfil these criteria? Why might he be at a disadvantage here because of his background?

This activity should take you about 40 minutes.

Discussion

Roberts writes that the interviewer has certain hidden assumptions about the interview, and that these 'serve to construct inequality when there is no shared definition of the interview'. In other words, although the interviewer has a set understanding of the genre and of what she expects to hear in the answers of a good candidate, the candidate himself is not in possession of this knowledge. The two parties in this interaction don't share the background understanding of what constitutes a successful interview, and because of this, the interviewee is at a distinct disadvantage. So, for example, the opening question is meant to give Ire a chance to talk about how he is able successfully to manage his own work ('self-management' is one of the 'key competencies'). But he is not asked about this in an explicit way, and so he doesn't realise that this is what he is meant to be demonstrating in his answer. Part of the reason that he doesn't share the same expectations about the genre as the interviewer is that these are conventions that are current in British interviews, but may not be the same in Ire's home culture of Nigeria. So although the interview is intended to be a fair and neutral assessment of any candidate's potential, instead it ends up being biased towards those who share the same knowledge of genre conventions as the interviewer.

2.4   Comic voices

What happens, then, when expectations about genre or register are broken? In an interview situation, if one mistakes the generic conventions the result will probably be a failure to get the job. In other words, the consequences of not following the (implicit) rules are a breakdown of communication. In some contexts, however, flouting the conventions can be part of the overall act of communication. For example, contravening generic expectations is a device that is often used in the construction of comedy.

Henri Bergson (1859–1941), the French philosopher, who wrote a famous treatise on the nature of comedy (*Laughter: An Essay on the Meaning of the Comic*), suggests that 'A comic effect is always obtainable by transposing the natural expression of an idea into another key' (2004 [1911], p. 61). We can think of the 'natural expression of an idea' as the conventional genre associated with an idea. To transpose it 'into another key' would be to shift from the expected to an unexpected genre or register. Purposefully flouting generic expectations, then, can result in what is known as 'register comedy' (Attardo, 1994). This is where one type of register is juxtaposed with another to create something incongruous. Below is a short example from one of the Jeeves and Wooster stories by P.G. Wodehouse. In this extract Bertie Wooster finds himself in a quandary when a friend asks if he could do her a favour. He feels that agreeing to such a request is likely to lead to unwanted intrigue. His valet, Jeeves, is on hand to offer advice:

> 'If I might make a suggestion, sir?'
>
> 'Press on, Jeeves.'
>
> 'Would it be possible for you to go to Totleigh Towers, but to decline to carry out Miss Byng's wishes?'
>
> I weighed this. It was, I could see, a thought.
>
> 'Issue a *nolle prosequi*, you mean? Tell her to go and boil her head?'
>
> (Wodehouse, 1966, p. 28)

You may not be familiar with the term *nolle prosequi*, unless you have a knowledge of legal terminology. It is a legal concept that comes from the Latin phrase meaning 'refuse to pursue', and is used in common law

[handwritten margin note: not in harmony or keeping with the surroundings or other aspects of something]

to describe an application by the prosecution to discontinue criminal charges before the trial. As such, it is part of the register of a specific discourse community – the legal profession – and thus has a sense of formality to it. Bertie, however, undercuts the formal nature of his comment by following up with the phrase 'tell her to go and boil her head'. In terms of straightforward meaning, the two phrases are synonymous – they both mean to refuse to take part in the scheme. But they are poles apart in terms of register, and thus their juxtaposition seems startling, and produces a comic effect.

Let's look at another example of register comedy, a passage from *Hard Times* by Charles Dickens, which you will read in the next activity. In this scene, Mr Gradgrind is giving advice to his daughter, Louisa, about whether she should accept a proposal of marriage from Mr Bounderby (Figure 2.4). She has asked her father if she should make the decision based on whether or not she loves Mr Bounderby. Mr Gradgrind is a very practical-minded man who is used to engaging in the worlds of business and commerce. The question about love initially throws him, but he regains his composure and responds to his daughter with an analysis of the situation as he sees it.

You will study *Hard Times* in greater depth in Book 3.

Activity

Read Mr Gradgrind's response to Louisa in the passage below. As you read, think about how a clash of registers creates a sense of incongruity. What effect does this have on the serious topic at hand?

'Why, my dear Louisa,' said Mr. Gradgrind, completely recovered by this time, 'I would advise you (since you ask me) to consider this question, as you have been accustomed to consider every other question, simply as one of tangible Fact. The ignorant and the giddy may embarrass such subjects with irrelevant fancies, and other absurdities that have no existence, properly viewed – really no existence – but it is no compliment to you to say, that you know better. Now, what are the Facts of this case? You are, we will say in round numbers, twenty years of age; Mr. Bounderby is, we will say in round numbers, fifty. There is some disparity in your respective years, but in your means and positions there is none; on the contrary, there is a great suitability. Then the question arises, Is this one disparity sufficient to operate as a bar to such a marriage? In considering this question, it is not unimportant to take into account the statistics of marriage, so far as they have

Figure 2.4   Henry French, 'Louisa, my dear, you are the subject of a proposal of marriage that has been made to me', engraving for edition of *Hard Times* Household edition, *c.*1870, 13 × 18 cm. Photo: © Charles Dickens Museum.

yet been obtained, in England and Wales. I find, on reference to the figures, that a large proportion of these marriages are contracted between parties of very unequal ages, and that the elder of these contracting parties is, in rather more than three-fourths of these instances, the bridegroom. It is remarkable as showing the wide prevalence of this law, that among the natives of the British possessions in India, also in a considerable part of China, and among the Calmucks of Tartary, the best means of computation yet furnished us by travellers, yield similar results. The disparity I have mentioned, therefore, almost ceases to be disparity, and (virtually) all but disappears.'

(Dickens, 1995 [1854], pp. 97–8)

Discussion

The language and ideas that Mr Gradgrind uses are wholly inappropriate for the nature of the issue, and have the effect of transforming the serious topic into an absurd scene. He engages only in a statistical and economic analysis of the pros and cons of a marriage; what is entirely absent from his speech is the vocabulary of love or romance. And, apart from the opening 'my dear', there is no sign that this is a father speaking to his daughter. When you read the novel later in the module you will see the human consequences of this clash of approaches. For now though, the point to note is that Dickens illustrates the failure of Mr Gradgrind to appreciate the emotional needs of his daughter by giving the character a comically inappropriate response, which is articulated through a highly incongruous register of speech.

It is also worth adding that Dickens himself, as the writer of this passage, is playing with the possibilities of language to produce this effect. We talked at the beginning of the chapter of language being a tool that is used to get things done. Another metaphor we could perhaps use is of language as a toy – that is, something people can play around with, and act on, in a variety of creative ways.

Now let us look at a comic version of a real-life situation you came across earlier: the job interview. In the next activity you will read an extract from the script of an episode of *The Smoking Room*, a comedy series originally broadcast on the BBC in 2004. In this scene, three work-colleagues are on their break. One of them, Barry, is about to go for an interview for a promotion (Figure 2.5). The other two, Lilian and Robin, offer to help him prepare by giving him a practice interview.

Reading 2.4 is from the 'shooting script' for the sitcom, which is designed as a blueprint for the director and actors, rather than something to be read as a completed text in its own right. You'll have a chance to watch the actual scene in the last activity of this section.

Activity

Turn to Reading 2.4 and read the extract from the script of an episode of *The Smoking Room*. How does Barry negotiate the expectations of the interview genre?

Discussion

Barry negotiates them very badly. He appears unaware of what is expected of his answer, and instead goes off into a completely inappropriate rant about things that annoy him about the job. As this is a comedy, Barry's failure to appreciate the expectations of the genre is much more extreme than in the real-life example we looked at above. And it is the extreme nature of the clash of registers that produces the humour here. But central to both the real-life version and the comic

Figure 2.5   Jeremy Swift as Barry from *The Smoking Room*. Photo: © BBC Motion Gallery.

version is the fact that situations like this have specific rules about how the communication is organised, and that these rules form the framework in which the meaning of the encounters themselves then happen. The scene from *The Smoking Room* is comic because Barry's answer is woefully inappropriate; Ire's job application is borderline because he doesn't pick up on the cues to talk about his 'key competencies'.

The televised version of this scene is included in the film 'The discourse of job interviews' on DVD 2. In the film, Celia Roberts, the author of Reading 2.3, and Brian Dooley, the writer of *The Smoking Room*, discuss the generic structure of interviews.

This activity should take you about 40–50 minutes.

Activity

Now watch 'The discourse of job interviews' on DVD 2. Why did Dooley choose to use a mock interview as part of the dramatic action of his story?

Discussion

In the film, Roberts explains how the generic structure of interviews manifests itself in real-life scenarios, and how candidates need to understand the rules of the game if they are to be successful. Dooley says that he used the format of a mock job interview as part of the narrative for this episode because he feels it works both as a way of illustrating aspects of the personality of his characters and for providing comic possibilities within the story: as he says, 'interviews aren't really normal human conduct. So you don't get normal human behaviour arising from them'.

2.5 Structure and point of view

So far in this chapter we've looked at various ways in which the meaning of an utterance is determined in part by the structure of the language and the way the communication is organised. In this final section we'll look at one further way in which form and structure have an important bearing on the meaning of a text. Our focus here will be on how the choices we make about which words to use and what order to put them in are related to the *perspective* we have towards what we're describing.

A simple example of this is the adage that some people see the glass as 'half full', while others see it as 'half empty'. Both phrases refer to the same physical entity: a glass with a set amount of liquid in it. But the choice of words used to describe this entity indicates two different perspectives on it. The linguist Norman Fairclough refers to this as 'construing reality'. He suggests that the way we describe the world around us contributes to the way we see the world. And the consequence of this is that *no* way of describing the world is entirely neutral. Whenever we describe something, we make particular choices about the vocabulary and grammar we use, and these choices are related to our own specific point of view. In the case of the half full/half empty glass, the perspective is considered to be a sign of one's personality (optimist versus pessimist); but in other contexts it could be one's political point of view or one's system of beliefs.

This activity should take you about 30 minutes.

Activity

Now turn to Reading 2.5, which is from an essay entitled 'Language, reality and power' by Norman Fairclough. In this section of the essay, Fairclough gives an example of how choices over vocabulary play a role in construing the world. The example he picks is, as he notes himself, an extreme case, and it is one that can generate a lot of debate and controversy. What point is Fairclough making in this extract?

Discussion

Fairclough maintains that there is no hard-and-fast rule about exactly what type of behaviour constitutes terrorism. For this reason, the word 'terrorist' can be used to describe a range of people acting in different ways, in different contexts and with different motivations. Most people can probably agree on a general definition of the word, but there are instances when different people will interpret actions and events in different ways and thus apply the word to different events. When someone does use the word, though, it immediately classifies the person who is being referred to in a particularly uncompromising and censorious way. So using the word clearly indicates an individual's attitude towards the person and the act he or she has committed, and as such it operates as a political statement about their behaviour.

– severely critical of her.

It is not only choices about vocabulary that create a particular perspective on the way the world is represented. Other choices related to language can also contribute to this. For instance, the syntactical structure of a sentence can be used to foreground certain aspects of the meaning. If, for example, I say: 'The child broke the window with his ball', I am foregrounding the child and his actions. If, on the other hand, I say 'The window was broken by the child's ball', despite the fact that the event described is exactly the same, the actions of the child are now being downplayed. In the second version the window is the subject of the sentence, and thus the child's actions are not stressed as much in the syntax.

Another element that contributes to the perspective of a story is the way other people's words and opinions are reported. This is especially the case in news reports, where the telling of a story often relies on the accounts of participants or witnesses. For example, a report on a football match that includes quotes only from the manager of the losing team might give the impression that the game was marred by bad refereeing and that the final score was a result of a string of bad luck. If the report includes quotes only from the winning manager, on the other hand, the story would probably suggest that the stronger team secured a well-deserved victory.

In the activity below we'll look at an example of how different choices about the language used in the narration of a story give different perspectives on the same event. In early 2010 there was a collision in the Antarctic Ocean between a Japanese whaling ship and an anti-whaling boat belonging to protesters from the environmental group Sea Shepherd. Sea Shepherd said that its boat, the *Ady Gil*, was deliberately rammed by the Japanese ship, the *Shonan Maru No. 2*. The crew of the *Shonan Maru*, on the other hand, said that the anti-whaling boat suddenly slowed in front of it and that the collision could not be avoided.

This activity should take you about 30 minutes.

Activity

Below are the opening paragraphs from two newspaper articles reporting the incident described above. Article 1 is from the Japanese newspaper the *Asahi Shimbun*; Article 2 is from the Australian tabloid the *Daily Telegraph*. Read through the two accounts and consider the ways in which the articles give a different perspective on the incident. Think specifically about the language they use. How do the choices they make about vocabulary, about what aspects of the story they foreground and whose opinions they report, contribute to the overall impression they give of what happened?

Article 1 – *Japanese newspaper*

Whale ship collides with protest vessel

An anti-whaling vessel was heavily damaged but its crew were rescued after a collision with a patrol ship for Japanese research whalers in the Antarctic Ocean on Wednesday.

The Fisheries Agency said there was no major damage to the *Shonan Maru No. 2*, which struck the bow of the *Ady Gil*, a 26-ton vessel belonging to the U.S.-based Sea Shepherd Conservation Society, around 12:30 p.m.

Crew members of *Ady Gil* were rescued by another protest vessel sailing in the vicinity.

No crew members aboard the 712-ton *Shonan Maru No. 2* were injured.

'A series of obstructive activities by Sea Shepherd should not be tolerated because they constitute an extremely dangerous act that threatens the lives of the crew,' the agency said.

(*Asahi Shimbun*, 2010)

Article 2 – *Australian newspaper*

Japanese cut in half anti-whaling ship *Ady Gil*

Anti-whaling group Sea Shepherd have confirmed their ship the *Ady Gil* has been rammed and cut in half by Japanese whalers.

According to Captain of the *Steve Irwin*, Paul Watson, the *Ady Gil* – a $1.5 million carbon-fibre stealth boat – was rammed by one of the Japanese security ships.

Mr Watson, who is in charge of one of the three Sea Shepherd vessels trying to interfere with the Japanese whale hunt, told the *Daily Telegraph* the Japanese vessel *Shonan Maru No. 2* rammed the *Ady Gil* and tore off its bow.

'The vessel is taking on water,' he said. 'The captain is still trying to salvage what he can and save his boat. The other five crew members have been rescued.'

The crew were rescued by fellow Sea Shepherd ship the *Bob Barker*.

Capt Watson said the Japanese refused to respond to mayday calls and fled the scene.

The Federal Government is investigating the reports.

(*Daily Telegraph* (Australia), 2010)

Discussion

If we start by comparing the two headlines we can immediately see a different perspective. Key to this perspective is the choice of verbs: 'Whale ship *collides* with protest vessel' and 'Japanese *cut in half* anti-whaling ship *Ady Gil*'. The former suggests something unplanned and maybe accidental; while the latter makes what happened sound much more deliberate. The *Daily Telegraph* article then follows this up by using the word 'rammed' to describe the collision, repeating the word in each of the first three paragraphs. Again, this gives the impression of an intentional and violent action. The *Asahi Shimbun*, on the other hand, repeats its far less evaluative description of a 'collision'.

The two articles also draw on different second-party accounts for the explanation of what happened. The *Asahi Shimbun* includes the opinion of the Japanese Fisheries Agency, while the *Daily Telegraph* quotes the captain of the Sea Shepherd boats. Unsurprisingly there appears to be a bias in both the accounts, which results in very different interpretations of the event. The captain contends that the Japanese refused to answer mayday calls, and that they fled after the incident. The spokesperson for the Japanese Fisheries Agency, on the other hand, argues that Sea Shepherd were and continue to be engaged in a series of obstructive activities, which are likely to endanger lives.

The result of the different choices made by the writers about the structure – from small decisions about individual vocabulary items to larger decisions about what to include and what to omit – is that the two articles could almost be about entirely different incidents, such are the discrepancies in the way they appear to see what happened. What is of interest to us, though, is not that different newspapers put different spins on the world, but the role played by language in the way they do this. Texts such as newspaper articles keep us informed about incidents in the world that we don't experience ourselves, and so in this sense we can say that language *mediates* the world around us. And given that much of our knowledge of the world comes from what we hear or read, paying attention to how language is used to represent the world can be an important act of critical awareness.

Conclusion

In this chapter we have looked at language being used for a diverse range of purposes – from telling stories about oatmeal, discussing stamp collecting and reporting on disputes over whaling, to providing commentary on baseball and cricket matches. The common thread throughout has been that the language used in any given context is tailored to the task to which it is being put, and that the form and structure of a piece of discourse is an important part of its meaning. In other words, there exist conventions about how language is used in different contexts and if we want to communicate effectively, we need to become familiar with these conventions and learn how to successfully exploit them. In the next chapter we'll continue our exploration of the process of communication by turning our attention to one particular type of language use – creative writing – and we'll examine some of the strategies, conventions and techniques that creative writers use as part of the process of expression.

References

Asahi Shimbun (2010) 'Whale ship collides with protest vessel' [online], *Asahi Shimbun*, 7 January, http://www.asahi.com/english/Herald-asahi/TKY201001070206.html (accessed 17 March 2010).

Attardo, S. (1994) *Linguistic Theories of Humour*, Berlin, Mouton de Gruyter.

Bakhtin, M. (1986) *Speech Genres and Other Late Essays* (trans. V.W. McGee), Austin, TX, University of Texas Press.

Bergson, H. (2004 [1911]) *Laughter: An Essay on the Meaning of the Comic* (trans. C. Brereton and F. Rothwell), Rockville, MD, Arc Manor.

Daily Telegraph (Australia) (2010) 'Japanese cut in half anti-whaling ship *Ady Gil*' [online], *Daily Telegraph* (Australia), 6 January, http://www.dailytelegraph.com.au/news/national/japanese-sink-anti-whaling-ship-ady-gil/story-e6freuzr-1225816675305 (accessed 26 July 2010).

Dickens, C. (1995 [1854]) *Hard Times*, London, Penguin.

Dooley, B. (2004) 'Doo Di Dum Di Da', *The Smoking Room*, unpublished shooting script.

Fairclough, N. (2009) 'Language, reality and power' in Culpeper, J., Katamba, F., Kerswill, P., Wodak, R. and McEnery, T. (eds) *English Language: Description, Variation and Context*, Hounslow, Palgrave Macmillan.

Fordyce, T. (2009) 'England v Australia 2nd Test, Lord's, Day Five as it happened' [online], story from BBC Sport, 20 July, http://news.bbc.co.uk/sport1/hi/cricket/england/8158326.stm (accessed 26 July 2010).

Gee, J.P. (2005) *An Introduction to Discourse Analysis: Theory and Method*, Abingdon, Routledge.

Harris, B. (2009) 'Dodgers top Cards and ace Carpenter 5–3 in NLDS [online]', story from Associated Press, 7 October, http://seattletimes.nwsource.com/html/sports/2010021246_apbbncardinalsdodgers.html?syndication=rss (accessed 26 July 2010).

Plain English Campaign (2010) Plain English Campaign [online], http://www.plainenglish.co.uk/ (accessed 26 July 2010).

Roberts, C. (2010) 'Institutional discourse' in Maybin, J. and Swann, J. (eds) *The Routledge Companion to English Language Studies*, Abingdon, Routledge.

Swales, J.M. (1990) *Genre Analysis*, Cambridge, Cambridge University Press.

Wittgenstein, L. (1953) *Philosophical Investigations* (trans. G.E.M. Anscombe), Oxford, Blackwell.

Wodehouse, P.G. (1966) *Stiff Upper Lip, Jeeves*, London, Penguin.

Further reading

Crystal, D. (2007) *How Language Works*, London, Penguin.

Culpeper, J., Katamba, F., Kerswill, P., Wodak, R. and McEnery, T. (eds) (2009) *English Language: Description, Variation and Context*, Hounslow, Palgrave Macmillan.

Robins, R.H. (1997) *A Short History of Linguistics*, London, Longman.

Readings

Reading 2.1: An example of a discourse community

The discourse community is a hobby group and has an 'umbrella organization' called the Hong Kong Study Circle, of which I happen to be a member. The aims of the HKSC (note the abbreviation) are to foster interest in and knowledge of the stamps of Hong Kong (the various printings, etc.) and of their uses (postal rates, cancellations, etc.). Currently there are about 320 members scattered across the world, but with major concentrations in Great Britain, the USA and Hong Kong itself and minor ones in Holland and Japan. Based on the membership list, my guess is that about a third of the members are non-native speakers of English and about a fifth women. The membership varies in other ways: a few are rich and have acquired world-class collections of classic rarities, but many are not and pursue their hobby interest with material that costs very little to acquire. Some are full-time specialist dealers, auctioneers and catalogue publishers, but most are collectors. From what little I know, the collectors vary greatly in occupation. One standard reference-work was co-authored by a stamp dealer and a Dean at Yale; another was written by a retired Lieutenant-Colonel. The greatest authority on the nineteenth century carriage of Hong Kong mail, with three books to his credit, has recently retired from a lifetime of service as a signalman with British Rail. I mention these brief facts to show that the members of the discourse community have, superficially at least, nothing in common except their shared hobby interest …

The main mechanism, or 'forum' for intercommunication is a bi-monthly Journal and Newsletter, the latest to arrive being No. 265. There are scheduled meetings, including an Annual General Meeting, that takes place in London, but rarely more than a dozen members attend. There is a certain amount of correspondence and some phoning, but without the Journal/Newsletter I doubt the discourse community would survive. The combined periodical often has a highly interactive content as the following extracts show:

2. Hong Kong; Type 12, with Index

No one has yet produced another example of this c.d.s. that I mentioned on J.256/7 as having been found with an index letter 'C' with its opening facing downwards, but Mr. Scamp reports that he has seen one illustrated in an auction catalogue having a normal

'C' and dated MY 9/59 (Type 12 is the 20 mm single-circle broken in upper half by HONG KONG). It must be in someone's collection!

3. The B.P.O.'s in Kobe and Nagasaki

Mr. Pullan disputes the statement at the top of J.257/3 that 'If the postal clerk had not violated regulations by affixing the MR 17/79 (HIOGO) datestamp on the front, we might have no example of this c.d.s. at all.' He states that 'By 1879 it was normal practice for the sorter's datestamp to be struck on the front, the change from the back of the cover occurring generally in 1877, though there are isolated earlier examples'; thus there was no violation of regulations.

My own early attempts to be a full member of the community were not marked by success. Early on I published an article in the journal which used a fairly complex frequency analysis of occurrence – derived from Applied Linguistics – in order to offer an alternative explanation of a puzzle well known to members of the HKSC. The only comments that this effort to establish credibility elicited were 'too clever by half' and 'Mr Swales, we won't change our minds without a chemical analysis'. I have also had to learn over time the particular terms of approval and disapproval for a philatelic item such as 'significant', 'useful', 'normal', and not to comment directly on the monetary value of such items.

Apart from the conventions governing articles, queries and replies in the Journal/Newsletter, the discourse community has developed a genre-specific set of conventions for describing items of Hong Kong postal history. These occur in members' collections, whether for display or not, and are found in somewhat more abbreviated forms in specialized auction catalogues, as in the following example:

1176   1899 Combination PPC to Europe franked CIP 4 C canc large CANTON dollar chop, pair HK 2 C carmine added & Hong Kong index B cds. Arr cds. (1) (Photo) HK$1500.

Even if luck and skill were to combine to interpret PPC as 'picture postcard', CIP as 'Chinese Imperial Post', a 'combination' as a postal item legitimately combining the stamps of two or more nations and so on, an outsider would still not be in a position to estimate whether 1500 Hong Kong dollars would be an appropriate sum to bid.

However, the distinction between insider and outsider is not absolute but consists of gradations. A professional stamp dealer not dealing in Hong Kong material would have a useful general schema, while a member of a very similar discourse community, say the China Postal History Society, may do as well as a member of the HKSC because of overlapping goals.

The discourse community I have discussed meets all ... the proposed defining criteria: there are common goals, participatory mechanisms, information exchange, community specific genres, a highly specialized terminology and a high general level of expertise.

Source: Swales, J.M. (1990) *Genre Analysis*, Cambridge, Cambridge University Press, pp. 27–9.

Reading 2.2: The problem of speech genres

We speak only in definite speech genres, that is, all our utterances have definite and relatively stable typical *forms of construction of the whole*. Our repertoire of oral (and written) speech genres is rich. We use them confidently and skillfully *in practice*, and it is quite possible for us not even to suspect their existence *in theory*. Like Molière's Monsieur Jourdain who, when speaking in prose, had no idea that was what he was doing, we speak in diverse genres without suspecting that they exist. Even in the most free, the most unconstrained conversation, we cast our speech in definite generic forms, sometimes rigid and trite ones, sometimes more flexible, plastic, and creative ones (everyday communication also has creative genres at its disposal). We are given these speech genres in almost the same way that we are given our native language, which we master fluently long before we begin to study grammar. We know our native language – its lexical composition and grammatical structure – not from dictionaries and grammars but from concrete utterances that we hear and that we ourselves reproduce in live speech communication with people around us. We assimilate forms of language only in forms of utterances and in conjunction with these forms. The forms of language and the typical forms of utterances, that is, speech genres, enter our experience and our consciousness together, and in close connection with one another. To learn to speak means to learn to construct utterances (because we speak in utterances and not in individual sentences, and, of course, not in individual words). Speech genres organize our speech in almost the same way as grammatical (syntactical) forms do. We learn to cast our speech in generic forms and, when hearing others' speech, we guess its genre from the very first words; we predict a certain length (that is, the approximate length of the speech whole) and a certain compositional structure; we foresee the end; that is, from the very beginning we have a sense of the speech whole, which is only later differentiated during the speech process. If speech genres did not exist and we had not mastered them, if we had to originate them during the speech process and construct each utterance at will for the first time, speech communication would be almost impossible.

...

Many people who have an excellent command of a language often feel quite helpless in certain spheres of communication precisely because they do not have a practical command of the generic forms used in the given spheres. Frequently a person who has an excellent command of speech in some areas of cultural communication, who is able to read a scholarly paper or engage in a scholarly discussion, who speaks very well on social questions, is silent or very awkward in social conversation. Here it is not a matter of an impoverished vocabulary or of style, taken abstractly: this is entirely a matter of the inability to command a repertoire of genres of social conversation, the lack of a sufficient supply of those ideas about the whole of the utterance that help to cast one's speech quickly and naturally in certain compositional and stylistic forms, the inability to grasp a word promptly, to begin and end correctly (composition is very uncomplicated in these genres).

Source: Bakhtin, M. (1986) *Speech Genres and Other Late Essays* (trans. V.W. McGee), Austin, TX, University of Texas Press, pp. 78–9, 80.

Reading 2.3: Institutional discourse

I:	right what would you tell me is the advantage of a repetitive job (1)	1
C:	advantage of a	
I:	repetitive job (1)	
C:	er I mean the advantage of a repetitive job is that er:m it makes you it it keeps you going, er it doesn't make you bored, you don't feel bored you keep on going and, I mean I me-a – and also it it puts a smile on your face you come in it puts a smile on your face you feel happy to come to the job the job will (trust) you	5
I:	you don't get to know it better	
C:	sorry	10
I:	you don't get to know it better	
C:	yeah we get to know the job better we I mean we learn new ideas lots of new ideas as well	
I:	right what is the disadvantage of a repetitive job	
C:	well, disadvantage er:m, er disadvantages (1) you may you may f-offend customers you may f-offend our customers in there that's a disadvantage of it	15
I:	you don't find it boring	
C:	yeah it could also be boring, to be boring and you- and you, yet by being bored you may offend the customers	20
I:	how how would you offend them by being bored	
C:	by not putting a smile on your face	

(Roberts and Campbell 2005: 39)

[Transcript conventions: I = interviewer; C = candidate; : lengthening of a sound; (1) silence timed in seconds]

This short extract exemplifies many of the themes of the selection interview. First, the hidden assumptions of the interviewers serve to construct inequality when there is no shared definition of the interview. Shared inferential processes depend upon 'socially constructed knowledge of what the interview is about' (Gumperz 1992: 303) but there are few explicit clues to this or what candidates' roles and modes of communicating should be. The question in line 1 is designed to elicit a particular competence that relates to self-management. British interviews are now routinely constructed around a competency framework that also includes competencies such as team working, communications, customer focus, adaptability and flexibility. These reflect the discourses of the 'new work order' (Gee *et al.* 1996) in which workers, however low their status in the workplace, are expected to buy into a corporate ideology. Flattened hierarchies require individuals to be autonomous and self-regulating. So the competency questions at lines 1 and 14 are based on a set of conventionalised expectations that repetitive jobs are boring, but that enterprising, self-managing candidates will recognise this and find ways of dealing with the boredom which will maintain their identity as motivated workers. The candidate's requests for clarification, the perturbation phenomena in lines 4 and 5 and the interviewer's rebuttals of his responses in lines 9 and 18 show that he has not cued into the special line of inferencing embedded in this new work order ideology and into the fabric of the interview …

… Despite Ire's best attempts to interpret the interviewer's questions, he remains a borderline candidate since the misunderstandings displayed create uncomfortable moments that feed into doubts about his acceptability for the job.

The sequential organisation of the interview illustrates its fundamentally asymmetrical character and the role of the interviewer in the final decision-making. Candidates are routinely blamed for what is a joint production (Campbell and Roberts 2007). The interview is controlled almost entirely by the interviewers who govern the interactional norms, allocation of turns and speaking roles (Komter 1991; Birkner 2004). In this extract, the interviewer has a script which she drives through and in which only certain answers are allowable and institutionally processable.

References

Birkner, K. (2004) 'Hegemonic struggles or transfer of knowledge? East and West Germans in job interviews', *Journal of Language and Politics*, vol. 3, no. 2, pp. 293–322.

Campbell, S. and Roberts, C. (2007) 'Migration, ethnicity and competing discourses in the job interview: synthesising the institutional and personal', *Discourse and Society*, vol. 18, no. 3, pp. 243–71.

Gee, J.P., Hull, G. and Lankshear, C. (1996) *The New Work Order: Behind the Language of the New Capitalism*, St Leonards, Allen & Unwin.

Gumperz, J. (1992) 'Interviewing in intercultural situations' in Drew, D. and Heritage, J. (eds) *Talk at Work*, Cambridge, Cambridge University Press, pp. 302–27.

Komter, M. (1991) *Conflict and Co-operation in Job Interviews*, Amsterdam, John Benjamins.

Roberts, C. and Campbell, S. (2005) 'Fitting stories into boxes: rhetorical and textual constraints on candidates' performances in British job interviews', *Journal of Applied Linguistics*, vol. 2, no. 1, pp. 45–73.

Source: Roberts, C. (2010) 'Institutional discourse' in Maybin, J. and Swann, J. (eds) *The Routledge Companion to English Language Studies*, Abingdon, Routledge, pp. 193–4.

Reading 2.4: Extract from shooting script of *The Smoking Room*

LILIAN   Let's get you ready now.

BARRY   How?

LILIAN   Do a dry run! We'll throw some awkward questions out – see how you cope.

BARRY REACTS.

Well … some questions.

…

SHE COMPOSES HERSELF FOR THE MOCK INTERVIEW.

So! I'm Sharon. [The name of their boss, who will be conducting the real interview.] She won't have a ciggy on the go. Obviously.

ROBIN AND BARRY NOD, WILLING HER TO HURRY ON.

Or such good legs!

SHE'S DISAPPOINTED THAT NONE OF THE MEN BACK HER UP ON THIS.

ROBIN   (*TO BARRY*) And you won't have your crossword.

BARRY   Oh. No.

IT SHOULD NOW BE APPARENT – IF IT HASN'T BEEN ALREADY – THAT BARRY USES HIS NEWSPAPER AS A SECURITY BLANKET. HE DOESN'T KNOW HOW TO SETTLE WITHOUT IT. HE TRIES FOLDING AND UNFOLDING HIS ARMS, ETC.

LILIAN   So, Barry. Thank you for attending this interview.

THERE'S NO RESPONSE FROM BARRY.

You should say something back.

BARRY	Like what?
ROBIN	'Ta'?
LILIAN	Would it help if he came in through the door?

BARRY MAKES TO RISE.

ROBIN	It's not *Peer Gynt*. Let's skip the first bit – that's just chit chat – he'll be fine with that.
BARRY	Will I?
LILIAN	Why exactly do you want this job?
BARRY	It's a lot more money and I get a desk right by the window.
LILIAN	You can't say that!
CLINT	He's keeping it real.
LILIAN	I think you should keep it unreal. Lie.

BARRY HAS A LONG THINK THEN CLEARS HIS THROAT.

BARRY   Well Sharon. It's not like I can't do the job. An orang-utan could do the job. If it was trained in powerpoint and excel. Only, I've always found there are two types of people who get ahead in this life. The first type, sadly, are back-stabbers, net-workers, users. The second I like to think of as … 'shithouses'. And I'm neither. I'm slow, steady Barry. Not the most dynamic of men. Necessarily. So I've had to sit back, watching the most unlikely people get promoted above my head. Promoted to the top in some cases. Well … one case. And it's a joke! Someone needs to stop the rot!

HE NOW REALISES THAT THIS SPEECH ISN'T GOING DOWN AT ALL WITH THE OTHERS.

And that's why I'd like this job.

IT'S A WHILE BEFORE LILIAN OR ROBIN CAN RESPOND.

LILIAN	Aah. You'll be fine.
ROBIN	Yeah, you'll walk it.

Source: Dooley, B. (2004) 'Doo Di Dum Di Da', *The Smoking Room*, unpublished shooting script, episode 2, scene 15, pp. 33–6.

Reading 2.5: An example of construing

How can we determine when people can be adequately construed as *terrorists*? This is currently sometimes a real problem, for journalists, politicians and ordinary citizens. We need some sense of what counts as *terrorism*, e.g., 'violence with a political and social intention, whether or not intended to put people in general in fear, and raising a question of its moral justification' (Honderich, 2003: 98–9), though not everyone will agree with this definition; and it helps to find clear cases most people could agree on – those who attacked the World Trade Center in New York in 2001 and the London Underground in July 2005 are perhaps pretty uncontentiously *terrorists*.

In some cases we might recognize that people use *terrorist* methods in something like Honderich's sense, and are *terrorists* in some sense, yet feel reluctant because of particular features of the context of their violence to leave it at that and so implicitly equate them with people who are *terrorists* in an unmitigated sense. This might be so with certain acts of extreme violence (e.g., suicide bombings) against Israeli civilians by Palestinians within the *intifada* (though I would unhesitatingly say that, for example, the Palestinians who murdered members of the Israeli team at the Munich Olympics in 1972 were *terrorists*) or by Iraqis in the aftermath of the Iraq War. This is because these actions can be seen as part of a war or insurgency, and are matched by and are responding to acts of comparable violence against civilians by military or paramilitary forces. Note that Honderich's definition is consistent with *state terrorism*, and we might ask why these Palestinians or Iraqis are widely called *terrorists* in the media whereas soldiers using *terrorist* methods are not. I sometimes feel that while such people are *terrorists* in a sense, this is not a fully adequate construal because they are resisting extreme violence, carried out by others who might equally be called *terrorists* but are generally not, so it is also inequitable, but I feel unsure what other word to use, what an adequate construal would be. It's difficult to grasp this bit of the world in language – that's the sort of difficulty we quite often have in construing the world, even if this is an extreme example of it.

[handwritten margin note: insurgent – a person fighting against a govt or invading force / rebel / revolutionary]

[handwritten margin note: organised similarly to a military force.]

Reference

Honderich, T. (2003) *After the Terror*, Edinburgh, Edinburgh University Press.

Source: Fairclough, N. (2009) 'Language, reality and power' in Culpeper, J., Katamba, F., Kerswill, P., Wodak, R. and McEnery, T. (eds) *English Language: Description, Variation and Context*, Hounslow, Palgrave Macmillan, p. 513.

3   Invented voices

Bill Greenwell

Contents

Aims

This chapter will:

- introduce you to some of the key principles of creative writing in prose
- develop your understanding of the way creative writing shapes and edits everyday language
- develop your understanding of how to create a voice in a story
- illustrate creative writing in action, by looking at some extracts from published texts
- offer you the opportunity to undertake brief exercises in creating and inventing voices.

Materials you will need

- DVD 2 (audio)

Introduction

In this chapter and the next one, you will be introduced to the academic discipline of Creative Writing, and specifically to ways in which voices are made by writers to 'speak' to a reader. In this chapter, you will be looking at prose and drama, and in Chapter 4, at poetry. You will encounter some examples of creative writing – and you will be asked to attempt some yourself.

3.1 Creative writing: purpose and process

Creative Writing is a discipline that is about process: you can't study it unless you try it, not least because the aim is to reflect on your writing at the planning stage, during composition and when you have finished.

As with the discipline of Literature, that of Creative Writing includes looking at existing texts. To a certain extent, it also analyses them. But the purpose of the analysis is quite different: it is to give you ideas of how you might write your own material; to give you a sense of what might or might not work for you as a writer; to understand the dynamic of writing in action. On a Creative Writing course of study you read a wide range of texts in order to think about strategies and tactics, rather than to analyse content and intention. In other words, it is about reading so that you can find and hone your own style, and about finding and honing the voices of characters and speakers you create. The examples of other people's writing will also give you reference points by which to analyse your own work. It is worth adding that practising original writing can not only be enjoyable in its own right, but can also enhance the way in which you study Literature, and indeed other subjects such as Classical Studies and Religious Studies – just as understanding the rudiments of how to cook can help you appreciate the skill that has gone into the making of a meal.

As a discipline, Creative Writing asks you to create stories or sequences of images, and to work through the best ways of engrossing a reader or **audience**. It asks you to look at generating ideas, and teaches you ways of refining language and structure so that these narratives or sequences have a maximum impact. One of the most important processes consists of **drafting** and editing what you have written, considering alternative ways of phrasing, and making decisions about such questions as what you need to leave in or leave out, and how best to sharpen the focus of what you write.

A good illustration of how editing can be used to sharpen the focus of a narrative is the experience of making a film. Whether for reasons of economy or for dramatic effect, film-makers rapidly learn how much they can leave out. If a film-maker wants us to know that a character is going from one place to another, for example, it may be tempting to **show** us the whole of the journey. However, if we see a character going in through the front door of an apartment block, say, on the way to an upstairs apartment, we do not need to see the character travelling up the stairs. In fact, we might not need to see the character going through the apartment door. Instead, a film-maker might simply take us directly from outside the front door to inside the apartment. The person inside might hear a rap on the door. Opening the door would reveal the character at the head of a stairwell. That would be enough to **tell** us that the character had made the journey. This kind of 'cut' is increasingly common in stories – and prose fiction has itself been much influenced by film. To get you used to this process of editing, the first activity asks you to edit a short and uninspiring piece of writing so that it is economical.

This activity should take you about 15–20 minutes.

Activity

Read the following passage, which I have invented, and which I have deliberately over-written. See how far you can edit it so that what happens is clear without having to be spelled out – that is, so that the content 'shows' what is happening, rather than 'tells'. You should aim to reduce it by 80–90 words, and, above all, make it more interesting. You may change or reorder any of the words, but keep the gist of the passage intact.

Molly ~~spread two slices of toast with raspberry jam, went over to the breakfast table, sat down in a chair, and ate them.~~ *sat at the breakfast table and ate her toast* She ~~looked through the window:~~ It was a sunny morning, ~~and it looked as if it would be a sweltering day, just as the weather forecast had predict~~ed. *and the forecast predicted a sweltering day* Her husband, ~~who was a gruff and surly type~~, sat opposite her, sucking his teeth in annoyance ~~at~~ *at what* ~~some item he wa~~s reading ~~in~~ the ~~daily~~ newspaper, ~~which they had delivered from the local shop.~~ He read out ~~some~~ extracts *to Molly* ˌHe was an arrogant man, the complete opposite of Molly, who was sensitive and lively, and who would have preferred a brighter conversation.

The phone rang in ~~the next room,~~ and Molly ~~got up, went over to the door, opened it, and~~ answered ~~it.~~ It was her daughter, Shelagh, ~~who had important and very shocking news to tell.~~ *calling to say* Her house had been burgled ~~the previous night,~~ *while they slept* ~~and some~~ valuable jewellery had been stolen ~~by the thief or thieves~~, including a locket ~~which~~ contained a picture of Molly's mother. Molly's mother had passed away twenty years earlier, but her memory ~~seemed very~~ *was* fresh in Molly's mind. She was instantly

upset, but let her garrulous daughter explain all the details of
the break-in, ~~which had happened, so her daughter said, when
she had been asleep~~. Molly asked her, when she could get a
word in, whether the police had been called.

Discussion

There are many examples in the piece of what might be termed poor or
clumsy writing, although the most glaring problem, I think, is the absence
of **dialogue**. It is uninhabited by the voices of characters, even if the
husband is 'a gruff and surly type' – something we would have realised if
we had heard him speak. We are also told that he is 'arrogant',
something it would have been better to find out for ourselves. Equally, we
didn't have to be told either that Molly is 'sensitive and lively' and later
that she is 'upset' or that the daughter is 'garrulous'. We could have
gleaned that from an excerpt of conversation or a description of
behaviour. We are told about the weather, when we could have had it
suggested; we are told pointless details, such as the process of sitting
down, the method of the newspaper delivery, the process of going to the
next room, and even that the news is 'shocking', which robs the news of
any shock. We are also told what happens in a relentlessly chronological
order, and given an indigestible chunk of **back-story** (about Molly's
mother). There is also some confusion about who 'she' is (there are three
women mentioned), and there is an unfortunate sequence of phrasing in
the very first sentence, which makes it seem as if the chair and table are
being eaten.

There are plenty of solutions, and one of the pleasures of writing is that
there is no perfectly right answer. Perhaps the best thing to do would be
to cut straight to the conversation between mother and daughter. The
opening line might be Molly saying 'What did they take?'. That would at
least force us to read on. Bringing a voice into a creative text is a good
way of enlivening it.

3.2   Voices and creative writing

In Chapters 1 and 2, you saw how speech works in various everyday contexts: how people use language, often very creatively, to communicate with one another. You will also be familiar with speech and conversation in fiction, in plays, in films, in poems and in **life writing**. ('Life writing' is the term used to cover both autobiographical and biographical writing.)

The first thing to recognise about a great deal of creative writing is that voices are, necessarily, representations or approximations of how people really talk. In prose fiction and drama, the aim is often to create an illusion of reality, to make you feel as if you are eavesdropping on the real thing. At the simplest level, this involves a degree of tidying up how people speak – removing some of the stutters, false starts, hiccups, even confusions that occur when people talk across each other. Speech in fiction and drama is edited.

As noted in Chapter 2, a transcript is a 'representation of speech'. Creative writers can use transcripts to fabricate scripts.

However, the main aims of speech are to give readers or audiences an insight into the character(s) and the action. Speech doesn't have the quality of a transcript – not least because a transcript can be quite dull, and relatively directionless. (We will come to ways of actually using transcripts for creative writing both later in this section and at the end of the chapter.)

The invented speech of fiction and drama is necessarily sharper and sometimes more evasive than it might be in 'real life', because the aim is to tell a story. And there is a further complication, too – what works in one genre may not work in another.

You have come across the term 'genre' in A150 in various contexts. In Creative Writing, as in Literature, 'genre' is used in two ways. It literally means (like 'genus' in science), a 'sort' or 'kind'. Creative Writing uses it to distinguish between poetry, drama, fiction and life writing. Each one is a 'genre'. However, 'genre' is often used, a little confusingly, to mean specific kinds of writing within the main genre, such as (in drama) screenplay, stage play, radio play, or (in fiction) crime, horror, romance, science fiction, fantasy, and so on. These divisions are sometimes known instead as 'sub-genres'. It may be the case that what works in the genre of fiction does not work in the genre of drama.

When the novelist and screenwriter Raymond Chandler adapted James M. Cain's *Double Indemnity* (1943) for Billy Wilder's 1944 film, he noted that Cain's dialogue was 'written for the eye not the ear' (MacShane, 1986 [1976], p. 107) – that is, it might work on the page, but it would sound wrong if heard out loud. Chandler rewrote the dialogue so that it suited the film. Or, as we might say, Chandler reinvented the language. In neither Cain's short novel nor in Chandler's script is the language a facsimile of how ordinary people speak. It approximates to it, but it edits and reshapes it. As Robin Cook, a novelist interviewed for Linda Seger's *Creating Unforgettable Characters* (1990), remarks, 'One of the amazing parts of really good dialogue is that it gives you the impression of being in the **vernacular** without being in the vernacular' (Seger, 1990, p. 168).

This is true even in the case of Harold Pinter, the British playwright and Nobel prize-winner whose early work for the stage was much commended for its verisimilitude. It was praised for its use of such devices as pauses (of different length), repetitions and linguistic confusions, as when a character in *A Night Out* (1960) claims that someone is 'very compressed', when he means 'depressed'. Yet Pinter's language was highly stylised. In fact, it's significant that the adjective 'Pinteresque' had made it into the *Oxford English Dictionary* within a few years of his first major stage success. Its definition of the word is 'Of or relating to Harold Pinter; resembling or characteristic of his plays', but adds 'Pinter's plays are typically characterised by implications of threat and strong feeling produced through colloquial language, apparent triviality, and long pauses.' In other words, Pinteresque language resembles the way Pinter writes: it doesn't mean that it is naturalistic. Other playwrights, notably Caryl Churchill, have experimented with overlapping dialogue. Churchill uses a backslash to indicate where speech overlaps, a device that has been widely adopted by other playwrights – but her work is often timed so that characters suddenly speak in unison: we get the 'reality' of people talking across each other, but the speeches are carefully constructed to coincide with and to echo one another. And the American playwright David Mamet, whose *Oleanna* (1993) begins with a telephone conversation, and with a speaker unable to finish his words, and whose trademark is bursts of unfinished, staccato sentences, sentences often thought of as 'realistic', has said that 'The language in my plays is not realistic but poetic. The words sometimes have a musical quality to them. It's language that is tailor-made for the stage. People don't always talk the way my characters do in real life, although they may use some of the same words … *It's an illusion*' (Kane, 2001, p. 49; my italics).

the appearance of being true or real.

Harold Pinter, Caryl Churchill and David Mamet

Harold Pinter (1930–2008) was the author of thirty plays, twenty screenplays and a variety of other writings. He won many awards, including the Nobel Prize for Literature. His first plays were produced in 1957, and his breakthrough came with *The Caretaker* in 1960. Martin Esslin wrote of the 'tape-recorder fidelity' of Pinter's dialogue, and noted that it was 'superficially at least, of a devastating naturalness … the vocabulary of real conversation … largely missed in stage dialogue that attempted to combine naturalness with good grammar, correct vocabulary and logical progression of its reasoning' (1963, p. 139). Pinter became particularly known for his use of the pause, as here in *The Caretaker*:

DAVIES	I was saying, he's … he's a bit of a funny bloke, your brother.
	MICK *stares at him.*
MICK	Funny? Why?
DAVIES	Well … he's funny …
MICK	What's funny about him?
	Pause.
DAVIES	Not liking work.
MICK	What's funny about that?
DAVIES	Nothing.
	Pause.
MICK	I don't call it funny.
DAVIES	Nor me.

(Pinter, 1977 [1960], pp. 49–50)

Caryl Churchill (b. 1938) is a playwright (for radio as well as stage), and has had more than forty plays produced, the most famous of which is *Top Girls* (1982). In her play *Three More Sleepless Nights* (1980), she decided she 'wanted two kinds of quarrel – the one where you can't speak and the one where you both talk at once. When I was writing *Top Girls* I first wrote a draft of the dinner scene with one speech after another and then realised it would be better if the talk overlapped in a similar way. Having got a taste for it I've gone on overlapping in most things I've written since' (Churchill, 1990 [1980], p. i).

Here are her instructions for *Three More Sleepless Nights*:

A speech usually follows the one before it BUT:

1) When one character starts speaking before the other has finished, the point of interruption is marked /

e.g.

MARGARET   I don't dislike him / but that don't mean I fancy him.

FRANK   And he don't dislike you. Eh? Has he said that? He don't dislike you? He don't dislike you.

2) A character sometimes continues speaking right through another's speech:

e.g.

MARGARET   Your friend. I don't like him /

FRANK   You fancy him.

MARGARET   like that, I quite like him.

(Churchill, 1990 [1980], p. 246)

David Mamet (b. 1947) is an American playwright and screenwriter, as well as a film director and critic. He has written more than twenty plays, and, including adaptations of his own stage plays, over twenty films – among his best-known works are *Glengarry Glen Ross* (1992) and *Oleanna*. His characters often speak in a staccato, half-finished fashion, as this extract from *Oleanna* suggests:

JOHN   (*Picks up paper.*) Here: Please: Sit down. (*Pause*) Sit down. (*Reads from her paper.*) 'I think that the ideas contained in this work express the author's feelings in a way that he intended, based on his results.' What can that mean? Do you see? What ...

CAROL   I, the best that I ...

JOHN   I'm saying, that perhaps this course ...

CAROL	No, no, no, you can't, you can't … I have to …
JOHN	… how …
CAROL	… I have to pass it …
JOHN	Carol, I:
CAROL	I *have* to pass this course, I …
JOHN	Well.

(Mamet, 1993, pp. 8–9)

In the next activity, you will look at how people actually speak in real life by reading an extract from a transcript of the '**Watergate**' tapes. These were recordings made of conversations in the Oval Office of the White House. The speaker here, H.R. (Bob) Haldeman, is talking to the Republican president, Richard Nixon, about a break-in at the Watergate Hotel, the headquarters of the Democratic Party, during the 1972 election campaign (Figure 3.1). Haldeman was Nixon's chief of staff, and, like other aides, was unaware that all conversations were being recorded. The recordings later led to Nixon's resignation.

Activity

Read the following extract from a transcript of the 'Watergate' tapes. As you read, think about why Haldeman's speech would fail to work in a play or a piece of prose fiction.

HALDEMAN   Okay – that's fine. Now, on the investigation, you know, the Democratic break-in thing, we're back to the – in the, the problem area because the FBI is not under control, because Gray doesn't exactly know how to control them, and they have, their investigation is now leading into some productive areas, because they've been able to trace the money, not through the money itself, but through the bank, you know, sources – the banker himself. And, and it goes in some directions we don't want it to go. Ah, also there have been some things, like an informant came in off the street to the FBI in Miami, who was a photographer or has a friend who is a photographer who developed some films through this guy, Barker, and the films had pictures of Democratic National Committee letter head documents and things. So I guess, so it's things like that that are gonna, that are filtering in. Mitchell came up with yesterday, and John Dean analyzed very carefully last night and concludes, concurs now with Mitchell's recommendation that the only way to solve this, and we're set up beautifully to do it, ah, in that and that ... the only network that paid any attention to it last night was NBC ... they did a massive story on the Cuban ...

PRESIDENT   That's right.

HALDEMAN   thing.

PRESIDENT   Right.

(Nixon and Haldeman, 1999–2002 [1972])

Figure 3.1   President Richard M. Nixon and his chief of staff, H.R. Haldeman, Oval Office, White House, Washington DC, *c.*1972. Photo: © Corbis.

Discussion

You have probably spotted that the speech here is too rambling to hold a reader's or an audience's attention. Almost at its outset, there is a complex sentence that piles up clauses, and alters the grammar as it goes along:

> Now, on the investigation, you know, the Democratic break-in thing, we're back to the – in the, the problem area because the FBI is not under control, because Gray doesn't exactly know how to control them, and they have, their investigation is now leading into some productive areas, because they've been able to trace the money, not through the money itself, but through the bank, you know, sources – the banker himself.

Even if I tell you what you might guess (that Gray is head of the FBI), you would, I suspect, have trouble understanding 'we're back to the – in the, the problem area' and 'they've been able to trace the money, not through the money itself, but through the bank, you know, sources – the banker himself' and 'So I guess, so it's things like that that are gonna, that are filtering in.'

Accuracy or fidelity to everyday speech is not the issue. We can tell that Haldeman is struggling with his thoughts, and he is after all addressing the president, so a degree of extra hesitation might be unsurprising. But fictional characters, created characters, have to communicate information not only to another character but also to an audience, and they may well have to communicate information about the story in which they 'exist'. If you were to dramatise or to fictionalise Haldeman's speech here, you would want not only to show him as anxious and uncertain, but also to make much clearer what he is talking about. That would mean, at the least, trimming away much of what he says, reducing his rambling. He is trying to suggest that the head of the FBI is not in control of events, and that this is potentially damaging to the president's authority. Perhaps he might be made to say

> The problem … the problem is that Gray can't control the FBI. They're finding out about the sources of the money. And that – that could mean – that could be difficult. For us. It could be very difficult.

This is a great deal more coherent than what was actually said, although notice that it uses some pauses, some repetitions and some hesitations. These are included to suggest the anxiety. They are also intended to mimic or to give the impression of some aspects of everyday speech: enough to convince a reader or a listener. My edit has also reduced the length of the speech. While it is perfectly possible for there to be lengthy passages of speech in drama or prose narrative, most speech is relatively short. This is because writing depends for the most part on being active, on possessing a forward movement.

3.3 Distinguishing one voice from another

Voices are crucial to writers, because voices mark characters out, and characters are at the heart of almost every good story. Nothing is more undramatic – or confusing – than having all the characters speak in exactly the same way. If you are watching a play, on screen or on stage, you can see who is speaking, of course, but it would still be tedious if everyone spoke in the same fashion: the way characters express themselves is the key to their identity.

When we make someone speak in a drama or prose fiction, we may of course be leading, or misleading, the reader as to what direction the story will take. The voice we provide may offer up facts: whole, partial or illusory. But for the moment, I would like you to concentrate on the process of creating a character through voice.

Activity

Suppose you are writing a story, in any medium or genre, and your character is explaining that he or she is late for an appointment or an event. Think of a few ways in which the character might admit to being late, and try to make what they say tell us something about their character and identity. One or two sentences for each character are all you need to create. When you have finished, look at my suggestions in the Discussion.

Discussion

Here are five possibilities:

(a) Late again, that's me!

(b) This watch has let me down all week: it's useless.

(c) Please may I apologise profusely for my tardiness. Inexcusable of me.

(d) How come it's always you that's on time, and never me?

(e) Okay, so I'm late. So what?

The speaker in Example (a) sounds like a bubbly, unapologetic, maybe even a slightly ditsy individual – an outgoing, happy-go-lucky type.

In Example (b) the speaker sounds impatient, disagreeable and ready to blame anyone or anything rather than apologise.

The speaker in Example (c) is formal: in fact, absurdly formal, perhaps pompous.

In Example (d), the speaker is probably an ironist, the kind of person who likes to make a joke out of life.

And the speaker in Example (e) seems blunt, to the point of rudeness.

Of course, the context in which the examples were spoken, or the intonation of the speakers, might change the way in which we interpret each of those lines. If the character habitually came out with these kinds of remark, though, we would begin to learn what to expect. (Remember however that, if these were the first encounters with the characters, the expectation might later be reversed.)

In the above examples, what matters is not the information that the character is late but the implied attitude of the speaker. This is because creative writing is nearly always concerned with building up character by indirect means: this is what allows readers and audiences to engage with the character and the story itself. There is no intrigue if a character arrives and announces 'I'm pompous' (which a pompous character is not likely to do). A pompous voice has to be established by the way it uses language, just as pompous characters have to be established by the actions they undertake. Equally important is what is not said, not undertaken.

Activity

Try the previous activity again, this time choosing a different subject and producing four examples of ways of making a statement, request or announcement about the same thing. You may choose any subject you like, but here are some suggestions.

Your character might be:

- complimenting someone on their appearance
- asking someone else to lend them some money
- making a marriage proposal.

Make some notes about the way your character comes across.

(enthusiastic)

Blimey - you look absolutely cracking!

Yeah, I think it hides most of your fat bits. *(jealous)*

It's nice. *(conceited)*

You look good but how about trying out a the black!

(closest friend).

Discussion

It might be helpful to test the lines on a friend, to see whether you have achieved the effect you hope for. You can do this in two ways – show them the remark on a piece of paper or read it out to them. It is best to let someone see or hear the different 'voices' one at a time. Bear in mind that reading them out loud will be hard to do without adding some idea of what you intended, because you are likely to add intonation.

3.4   The narrator's voice

In fiction and in life writing, stories are told. It is not merely the voices of the people in a story that engage a reader. When writing a story, you have to consider the narrative point of view from which the story is being told, and there are many different ways of intriguing a reader, depending on your strategy. You might use quite a neutral narrative voice, in which case the significance of voice passes to a greater degree to the characters. But equally you might tell the story from the point of view of one of the characters – someone who is directly involved in the action or on its periphery. A peripheral **narrator** is sometimes called a 'witness narrator' – one of the most famous being Nick Carraway in F. Scott Fitzgerald's novel *The Great Gatsby* (1925), who observes the actions of the other characters, but does not take a central part in the action.

Having a character tell the story is not at all unusual. Many pieces of fiction, and almost all autobiographical life writing, are told in the first person. The voice you give this first-person narrator is important, not least because it is likely to be biased or opinionated. First-person narrators may even be made 'unreliable': this is a device many creative writers have used in order to create tension in a story, forcing the reader to assess and reassess their own responses.

Activity

Here is the opening passage of *Tono-Bungay* (1909) by H.G. Wells (1866–1946). It is narrated by the central character, George Ponderevo. What do you make of Ponderevo, judging by his voice? Think about the tone of the voice, and also its rhythm.

> I have got an unusual series of impressions that I want very urgently to tell. I have seen life at very different levels, and at all these levels I have seen it with a sort of intimacy and in good faith. I have been a native in many social countries. I have been the unwelcome guest of a working baker, my cousin, who has since died in the Chatham infirmary; I have eaten illegal snacks – the unjustifiable gifts of footmen – in pantries, and been despised for my want of style (and subsequently married and divorced) by the daughter of a gasworks clerk; and – to go to my other extreme – I was once

– oh, glittering days! – an item in the house-party of a
countess. She was, I admit, a countess with a financial aspect,
but still, you know, a countess. I've seen these people at
various angles. At the dinner-table I've met not simply the
titled but the great. On one occasion – it is my brightest
memory – I upset my champagne over the trousers of the
greatest statesman in the empire – Heaven forbid I should be
so invidious as to name him! – in the warmth of our mutual
admiration.

And once (though it is the most incidental thing in my life) I
murdered a man ...

(Wells, 1972 [1909], pp. 9–10)

Discussion

You may have sensed that this is a narrator in a hurry, a character from
whom words spill with prodigal speed. The way the speaker switches
subjects so rapidly, and interrupts himself with asides, such as 'oh,
glittering days!' and 'it is my brightest memory', combine to suggest
someone who is intense, upbeat, on the verge of being boastful. Perhaps
you might think this egotistical strain in the voice is mitigated by a sense
of impish, candid glee. Wells enjoys teasing the reader, too – there is
something quite calculated about Ponderevo's chatter, not least in the
way he refers, mock-casually, to murder as 'incidental' in the last,
elliptical line. That he uses the word 'I' fourteen times in only 214 words
suggests that he loves the sound of his own voice. And the rhythm is
driven, energetic, hectic, as if the narrator is something of a gas-bag.
Importantly for a fictional voice, he makes you want to read on, and
follow him as 'urgently' as he says he is explaining himself. It has the
patter, I would say, of a spoken voice: a sort of intimacy, although
deliberately coy.

The next activity gives you the opportunity to try your hand at building
up a character by creating a fictional voice.

Activity

Now see if you can write 100–200 words of 'voice' that create a character. Remember, it is important not to be direct about the character's qualities – these should be implied by the way the character speaks.

This activity should take you about 15–20 minutes.

Discussion

You will probably have found this activity easier to achieve if you did not start with a set idea in your mind. It is best to think of a situation in which to place your character, and to see how the character develops. Although creative writing entails forward planning, the early stages – finding voices, finding characters – is best achieved by discovering the voice or character as you go, and editing what you have done afterwards.

3.5   Narrators and characters

Now, you will look at a short story in which the narrator is one of (three) characters. You will focus on two aspects – how the narrator speaks when she is narrating, and how the characters (including the narrator) speak to each other. You should be alert to the way the writer, Mary Robison (b. 1949), has developed the voices, and think about how she hopes or expects that the reader will react. Plainly, a story involves much more than voice – it involves structure, time, theme, plot (the ordering of the events in the story). The characterisation will come from what the narrator and characters do as well as what they say.

This activity should take you about 45 minutes.

Activity

Turn to Reading 3.1 and read 'Pretty Ice' by Mary Robison. It will be best to read the story twice – in the first instance, simply read through it as you would with any story. After this go back, and see what details you notice about how the narrator and the characters speak, and what these details reveal.

Discussion

Did you spot how appropriate the title, 'Pretty Ice', is to Robison's narrator, Belle? From the outset, Belle is frosty. There is something tetchy about how she depicts the intrusion her fiancé's arrival represents (she is more interested in her accounting). She dislikes her mother's 'compact' car, complains about her own new shoes, is grumpy about the tyre on her mother's car, about her mother's humming, the 'girlish' extra weight put on by Will, the way her mother accidentally honks the horn, the ink-spots on Will's mouth, her mother's suggestion that Will stay in Belle's old room, the way her mother gets lost. In fact, the writer has used Belle's voice to depict her as hostile and negative. (What is skilful about the story is that we are given the option of attributing this to lack of sleep, before discovering that the likely cause is her father's suicide fourteen years earlier, and allowing us to hazard that he, like Belle, has been something of a depressive.) Notice how much of the strength of this story comes from Robison's manipulation of Belle's voice. When a creative writer is developing a voice, the voice needs to be consistent in tone, in what we might call attitude.

In the next section, we will return to Robison's story, looking in particular at dialogue, and how this can be developed.

3.6 Dialogue

'Dialogue', in creative writing, is the term we give to what takes place when two or more characters are speaking. It is fairly rare to find several characters talking in the same scene, even when there are many characters in a novel, play or film. It is rarer still on radio (because it is difficult for listeners to follow) and also rare in short stories, which tend to focus on a few characters and a relatively short space of time (as 'Pretty Ice' does).

As noted in Section 3.2, dialogue never copies real-life conversation. It simply takes on the air of real-life conversation. The novelist and screenwriter Sol Stein makes this point (Stein is often aggressively assertive, as this extract suggests):

> If you need proof that dialogue and spoken words are not the same, go to a supermarket. Eavesdrop. Much of what you'll hear in the aisles sounds like idiot talk. People won't buy your novel to hear idiot talk. They get that free from relatives, friends, and at the supermarket.
>
> (Stein, 2003, p. 113)

As Stein observes, good dialogue in a story (for any medium) needs to be 'oblique' – that is, to contain indirect responses. You might think that Stein is overstating the case, and I would agree that it is easy to derail writing by never creating a straightforward conversation. But I think Stein is crucially right about the opening sallies in fictional dialogue. This does not mean that every line has to stray in a surprising direction, but it does mean that platitudes need to be avoided – perhaps especially at the outset of a scene. In 'Pretty Ice', there are exchanges that would look like this if laid out as a script for a play or film:

BELLE I think you're getting a flat. That retread you bought for the left front is going.

MOTHER I finally got a boy I can trust, at the Exxon station. He says that tire will last until hot weather.

and

MOTHER Why doesn't Will stay at my place, in your old room, Belle? I'm all alone there, with plenty of space to kick around in.

BELLE We'll be able to get him a good motel.

In the first exchange, notice how Mother does not exactly answer Belle, and in the second exchange, how Belle diverts her away from the question entirely. The dialogue in 'Pretty Ice' moves away from 'real' conversation in the way it is edited and presented to us by the writer. The exchanges are not there to replicate small talk but to invite us to speculate about character. Nor does Robison, in either case, use any verb other than 'said' (although she does say that Belle says the line about the motel 'quickly, before Will could answer'. Arguably, Robison does not need even to add this qualification. The words themselves imply it).

In getting us to speculate about character, of course, Robison is advancing the story, since it is a fundamental of most good storytelling that character drives it. And one of the principal ways of defining a character in a text is by his or her voice.

Activity

Imagine an exchange between two characters, in which the first character's opening line is:

How are you doing?

See if you can come up with a riposte to this relatively harmless-looking opening remark – a riposte implying that there is more going on in the exchange, and that there is more to find out.

Discussion

An answer like 'Very well, thank you' will stop any piece of writing dead in its tracks. A more intriguing answer would be indirect, evasive, or (superficially) not apparently an answer at all. Think about the following suggestions, and compare them with your own.

Exchange (a)

FIRST CHARACTER How are you doing?

SECOND CHARACTER You haven't heard what they say.

Exchange (b)

FIRST CHARACTER   How are you doing?

SECOND CHARACTER   I see you have a new friend.

Exchange (c)

FIRST CHARACTER   How are you doing?

SECOND CHARACTER   It looks as if one of us is in trouble.

In each exchange, the innocuous opening conversational gambit is derailed by the reply. This is not to imply that creative dialogue consists of characters refusing to answer questions, or being deliberately obtuse. A conversation that consisted entirely of stand-offs would become tedious. All the same, dialogue has to do more than establish the act of speech. The interaction of the voices has to move a story on, and make the reader or audience want to move on with it. You may want to try repeating the activity with different opening lines, for example: 'Would you like a lift home?' or 'This is the first time I've been here'.

3.7 Subtext

In the activity in the previous section, you were creating not only text but **subtext**. Subtext is what the conversation beneath the words is communicating (both between characters, and to the reader/audience). The subtext, for instance, of Belle's remark to her mother about the supposedly faulty tyre in 'Pretty Ice' is that Belle considers her mother to be generally incompetent. It might also be said to mean 'You irritate me, as ever'.

A much cited comment on subtext occurred in Harold Pinter's speech in 1962 to the National Student Drama Festival, at a time when his plays were repeatedly described as being about 'a failure of communication':

> There are two silences. One when no word is spoken. The other when perhaps a torrent of language is being employed. This speech is speaking of a language locked beneath it ... *The speech we hear is an indication of that which we don't hear.* ... I think that we communicate only too well, in our silence, in what is unsaid, and that what takes place is a continual evasion, desperate rearguard attempts to keep ourselves to ourselves.
>
> (Pinter, 1991, p. xiii; my italics)

Notice that Pinter refers to two kinds of subtext – the implication of characters not speaking, and there being silence; and the implication of what they actually mean when they are speaking. While Pinter might be regarded as having made the art of meaningful silence his own, he is making an important point. What a character says does not necessarily coincide with what he or she means.

One clear and comic example of subtext occurs in Woody Allen's film comedy *Annie Hall* (1977), when the two characters Alvy (Woody Allen) and Annie (Diane Keaton) first meet. The exchange between them is accompanied on-screen by subtitles, shown below in italics, which show what they are really thinking. They are talking about photography.

ALVY   They're ... they're ... they're wonderful, you know. They have ... they have, uh ... a ... a quality.

(You are a great-looking girl)

ANNIE   Well, I-I-I would – I would like to take a serious photography course soon.

(He probably thinks I'm a yo-yo)

ALVY   Photography's interesting, 'cause, you know, it's – it's a new art form, and a, uh, a set of aesthetic criteria have not emerged yet.

(I wonder what she looks like naked?)

ANNIE   Aesthetic criteria? You mean, whether it's, uh, a good photo or not?

(I'm not smart enough for him. Hang in there)

(Allen and Brickman, 2000, pp. 39–40)

What we have here is both an acknowledgement and a parody of ~~subtext~~ *an emulation of the* (which can be much more complex than Allen's examples). *style of a particular writer, not a*

When writing creatively, in any genre, it is <u>important to have some</u> *genre with* <u>sense of the subtext</u> in your head. What is your character really saying? *deliberate* Perhaps it is important here to say that you do not need to have an *exaggeration* absolutely precise interpretation in your head, or a parallel set of statements that constitutes the subtext. As the screenwriter Jules Feiffer remarks in an interview (Seger, 1990, p. 171),

> Working with subtext is not a matter of working it out with notes on it. It's a matter of understanding perfectly <u>what's really going</u> on, <u>what's not going on</u> and <u>why it's not</u>, and how much of it will <u>show on the surface</u> … You have to <u>leave some</u> [of the subtext] <u>for the audience to work out for itself</u> … as a member of an audience [I] love to be forced to think and be challenged.

In the same interview, Feiffer remarks that he has 'often been surprised by what my characters have had to say to each other. You get them going and they take off on their own'. Many <u>writers discover</u> their <u>characters</u> in the process of creating them. And writers of scripts for stage, screen or radio <u>give their scripts to</u> actors and directors for interpretation, just as writers of fiction, non-fiction and poetry surrender their voices to readers.

Figure 3.2 Scene from *Three More Sleepless Nights* by Caryl Churchill, featuring Paul Ready and Lindsey Coulson. National Theatre, London 2009. Photographed by Richard Hubert Smith. Photo: © Richard Hubert Smith.

This activity should take you about 15–20 minutes.

Activity

Read the following extract from Caryl Churchill's short play *Three More Sleepless Nights*. In it, a couple, Margaret and Pete, are discussing Margaret's previous relationship, with her husband Frank (Figure 3.2). What do you think they are really saying to each other? What possible subtexts does the exchange between them contain? There are several ways you might set about this task, including reading it with a friend, and annotating the text.

MARGARET   I was so insecure, that was part of it.

PETE   You had no life of your own.

MARGARET   I was just his wife. I wasn't a person.

PETE   You can't blame him though, I mean.

MARGARET   I don't. I don't any more. I'm sorry for him.

PETE   Yes, I'm sorry for him.

MARGARET   He's still drinking. He hasn't changed.

PETE   You're the one who's changed.

MARGARET   I've changed. I was just his wife before. I had no life.

(Churchill, 1990 [1980], p. 266)

Discussion

There are many ways of reading this extract, as actors would have to do. (It is true that it would be easier in the context of the whole play, but every line does need some close attention.) As perhaps you have noticed, the dialogue here is interesting because it is a little unpredictable – as when Pete says 'You can't blame him', after apparently having begun by echoing Margaret's words. You may well have questioned the extent of Pete's sincerity. And you may have noticed that the text shows us that the voices are distinctive: Margaret is more animated, Pete rather laconic. In part this is because Pete only gives us single sentences. The pattern of their language is different. There is a contrast between the two characters – important in any medium.

The contrast is what Churchill, as a writer, has provided. As a playwright, even though she has in her career frequently worked closely with directors and actors at the formative stage of her plays, Churchill is working in a genre that obviously involves handing over her material for interpretation. She cannot be present at every performance, advising 'I meant it to be said like this.' She has to allow not only the actors but an audience their freedom.

3.8   Subtext and prose fiction

Less obvious, but just as important, is that creative writers in other genres – in prose, in poetry – also have to reach a stage in which they hand over their voices and texts for interpretation: by readers. You can indicate a subtext as a writer, and it is important that you do, but you cannot reach the stage where a reading of your voices and texts is definitive. Readers bring their own experiences and prejudices and personalities to a text.

The solution might be for prose writers to add more direction, for instance by the use of verbs and adverbs. We could take the first line above, and transpose it into prose as follows:

poor example

'I was so insecure, that was part of it,' murmured Margaret wistfully, the tears beginning to well up in her eyes.

tearful [given to weeping

The trouble is that, once you, via your narrator, interpret the voices for the reader, your text will start to become unwieldy. It will be so filled with signals that you will crowd your reader out. The sentence I've just created is a very poor one, because it not only tells you that it is murmured, but also that it is wistful, and that it is practically lachrymose (and, incidentally, notice how 'in her eyes' is redundant – tears have nowhere else to well up). Having a sense of your subtext is important, but repeatedly defining it for the reader is to be avoided – a prose writer, like a dramatist, has to relinquish ownership.

This activity should take you about 20–25 minutes.

Activity

Create a short dialogue between two people (two contributions from each) in which what they say is not precisely what they mean. It doesn't matter whether you do this in the style of fiction or as a piece of drama. When you have finished, write down what you think was going on underneath the conversation – in the subtext. You might choose to do this the other way round, incidentally – write the subtext first, and then turn it into dialogue.

Discussion

One thing you will notice immediately is that this is harder to do in prose than it is in stage or film drama. In drama, fewer words will usually be required, because the actors – whether instructed to do so by a stage direction, or by a director, or through their own interpretation – will be able to hint at subtext by using body language, and by altering the tone and timbre of their voices. In film, because of the use of close-ups, it is possible to have significant 'conversations' with very few words being spoken.

As an actor and director, the American star Clint Eastwood has made a career out of 'speaking silences', as has the French actor Isabelle Huppert. Sometimes quite banal dialogue (as it may seem on the page) can be highly charged in film. In prose fiction, you have to supply the context, and give us some insight into what the character may be thinking. As noted above, you don't have to use adverbs and powerful verbs to do this. You can use a narrative technique which allows you to look into a character's head, and to hear their thoughts – in effect, a kind of subtext being brought to the surface for the reader's inspection. Here is an invented example:

'Do you want to come with me to the station?'

'Of course.'

They climbed into the car. It was not, Sarah knew, the wisest decision. Her father would use the journey to start one of his interminable debates about why women, and Sarah's mother in particular, were addicted to shopping. But why shouldn't her mother go shopping? She heard her father clearing his throat for a predictable monologue. She would let it all wash over her.

We are seeing here what Sarah really thinks: 'But why shouldn't her mother go shopping?' We don't even need the phrase 'she thought'. It is worth adding that this technique, which is called **free indirect speech**, is often unsuccessful when a writer attempts to let us look into the thoughts of more than one character in a story.

3.9   Voices from real life

Faithfulness

Life writers – autobiographers and biographers – have an interesting challenge in that, when they are creating the voices of people who actually lived, or are living, they have to <u>achieve a degree of fidelity to the original</u>. Since none of us possesses perfect recall, the voices in (for instance) a conversation are going to have to be recreated. In effect, life writers have much the same task as writers of prose fiction: they have to edit any recreated dialogue so that the speech is believable, and gives an insight into character. A great deal of life writing sits interestingly on the fence between fiction and fact, and life writing is often distinguishable from fiction only by its stated intention. There are many novels that have been discovered later to have been highly autobiographical, and many autobiographies that have subsequently turned out to have played fast and loose with the truth. But prose life writing borrows the skills of structure, characterisation, narrative and voice from fiction.

This activity should take you about 45 minutes.

Activity

1   Turn to Reading 3.2, which is an extract from *Humping My Bluey* (1966), the autobiography of Graham McInnes (1912–70). In the passage McInnes describes an incident that occurred when he was sixteen, in Melbourne, in 1929. In what way does the dialogue seem constructed? What makes it work?

2   Think back to an incident from when you were sixteen. Write 200 words about the incident, and include a similar amount of dialogue.

Discussion

You probably found that, as with McInnes, you were obliged to invent the dialogue so that it approximated to any conversation that actually took place. I think we might guess that McInnes recollected a verbal set-to about his comments on the girl's pigtails, and reconstructed it so that it was entertaining. You might have noticed that the question-and-answer session between them is oblique, with statements being countered indirectly. The exchange

'What business is it of yours?'

'It makes you look like a little girl.'

is not straightforward. The question of 'what business' it is, is countered by an answer that might be construed as rude, and that perhaps implies a subtext 'I am trying to annoy you, and have no interest in your hair'. You might also notice that the dialogue here is framed by a passage that is in the present tense, making the past seem briefly more immediate.

3.10 Transcripts, oral history theatre and verbatim theatre

In this final section of the chapter, we will look at examples of life writing that have elected to remain faithful to what has been recorded and transcribed. 'Oral history' – the recording of voices by social historians, most notably Charles Parker – has a sixty- or seventy-year history: that is, over a period when equipment became portable, and from a time when the BBC radio services first became interested in presenting the language of dialect. Creative writers have found this process interesting and fruitful for a variety of reasons, just as the opening up of the Mass-Observation archives from the 1980s onwards has also led to numerous life writing anthologies and works of fiction. The M-O archive became available online in 2008.

Charles Parker

Charles Parker (1919–80) was a radio producer with the BBC who was a key figure in the creation of oral histories. He recorded the words of working men and women for radio programmes, most notably *Radio Ballads* between 1958 and 1963, in collaboration with the folk musicians Ewan MacColl and Peggy Seeger.

Mass-Observation

Mass-Observation (which still exists, although without its hyphen) was an organisation founded in 1937 by Tom Harrisson, Charles Madge and Humphrey Jennings to record the opinions of volunteer diarists on a range of social issues. Its archive is at the University of Sussex. It is of interest to creative writers as well as social historians: perhaps the most well-known product of its archive was *Housewife, 49* (2007), Victoria Wood's television adaptation of the diaries of Nella Last.

One of the attractions of recorded speech is the authority of authenticity. As you have seen in Book 1, authority can take a variety of forms. Many writers – especially film-makers – invest their works with authority by stating (or at any rate alleging) that the events to be witnessed are based on 'a true story'. Films such as *De-Lovely* (2004), a biopic of the composer Cole Porter, or *Pierrepoint* (2005), a portrait of Britain's most famous executioner, carry with them the cachet of 'truth'. It is not hard to show that both of them, like most films declaring themselves to be 'true' or 'based on truth', contain conflations, changes of focus or date, and inventions or distortions of actual fact. But that they carry extra authority because they claim to speak to us with a degree of truth is part of their appeal.

Hand-me together different elements

Oral history theatre and **verbatim theatre** are extremely conscientious about fidelity. 'Oral history theatre' is an overarching term used to describe drama that uses transcripts to a greater or lesser degree. 'Verbatim theatre' is a more specific term used of drama that is almost entirely constructed from transcripts and, occasionally, public documents.

The writer Rib Davis (b. 1952) has used material spoken by real people to create scripts for stage, radio and television. The next activity will give you the opportunity to look at how a transcript of a person's original words might be transformed into a piece of drama and hear how Davis approaches the task.

Activity

1   Read the transcript below, which describes a car crash. You can hear the transcript being read aloud in 'Unadapted text (Rib Davis)' on DVD 2.

2   Imagine that you have to present this story as a dramatisation of about between two and four minutes' duration in a stage play. What might you do to make it interesting for an audience? You can make some notes or, if you would prefer, produce a short piece of script.

3   Now listen to 'Dramatisation of text (Rib Davis)' on DVD 2; Reading 3.3 is the script of the dramatisation. When you have done this, listen to 'Interview with Rib Davis'. How has Davis transformed the transcript into a piece of drama?

This activity should take you about 40 minutes.

JILL   We were going like the clappers in this beaten-up old thing, I
       don't think it had ever done this speed in its life before, and
       Cherry had got her head out the window yelling at all the passers-
       by and Sheila and Penny were in the back shouting things like 'Is
       this all it can do?' 'Put your foot down' – but my foot was flat on
       the floor as it was, I mean we were determined to get to the
       cinema before the thing started and, well it was fun too, I mean it
       felt really great … all of us together … And then – well you
       know this – the tyre blew, the front tyre on the driver's side, and
       there wasn't time to say anything, not even … well I mean maybe
       someone said, 'Oh God' or something but I don't remember any
       screaming, though there may have been, I think we just sort of
       clung on – to whatever – just sort of clung on, and first we went
       all over the road and then we went off into this ditch and you
       could feel the balance going and we went over, and over, and
       over, and then we stopped … And then there was a moment, well
       I say a moment, I don't know how long it was – but thinking,
       'I'm still alive. I'm still here.' And then we all started checking
       that we *were* all there. And we were, God knows how, especially
       Cherry, who'd had her head out the window. She was in hospital
       for three months, traction, on her back, but she was alive. The
       front window, the windscreen, it came out in one piece – I
       suppose it's meant to do that, and we all crawled out of that. We
       didn't deserve to be alive, I suppose.

(Davis, 2008, pp. 186–7)

Discussion

There are about 300 words in the transcript, of which about half find their
way into the finished scene. Many of the other words are implied by or
even reproduced in the stage directions, e.g. 'together they turn over and
over'. Very occasionally a tense is changed: otherwise, what we have
here are the original words.

However, Davis has turned the original monologue into dialogue, shared
between four characters, who sometimes echo each other ('clung on …
clung on …'), and who sometimes address each other, and sometimes
address the audience. This device gives the script far greater energy, an
energy which you will note in the dramatisation on the DVD. Not only
that, the order in which the words taken from the transcript are used is
quite different. And they also come to us in brief sections (the longest
speech is only twenty-five words). What Davis has done is to dramatise

the transcript by editing it, by changing its context and by multiplying the voices. The repetitions and pauses have also been added to give the piece greater tension and drama (as have the actions, such as the mime of rolling over). The example here shows us that, while transcripts are often unwieldy, it is possible to use sections of 'real' language – by presenting it, edited, and by adapting it to fit the artifice of theatre. As Davis comments (2008, p. 189), 'In real life four women would never divide a sentence up between them like this ['We – were – going – like the clappers'], but this is theatrical dialogue, not real life.' You may have been tempted to present the original transcript as a single voice, perhaps edited. But a stage adaptation requires greater speed, more activity, more for the audience to focus upon.

What is interesting about Davis's work is that it operates with integrity: wherever possible, he involves those whose writing he has transcribed in the process of staging a play. Verbatim theatre takes further this concern to be faithful to the source material. Philip Ralph's play *Deep Cut* (2008), which concerns the alleged suicide of a young army private, Cheryl James, at Deepcut Barracks, takes great pains to use almost no word that cannot be found in the transcript of an interview, a newspaper, radio or television report, parliamentary records or in the text of the inquiry. Nevertheless, Ralph has a play to write. He may not alter the words, but he edits them together, conflates occasional characters and stitches the many excerpts together into a coherent whole. This should alert you to the fact that writing is very much a process of adaptation as well as imagination, as much about structure and editorial work as about inspiration. In *Deep Cut*, the performers speak actual words uttered by actual people, as set down in extant and public records: indeed, this is what gives the play, to return again to the theme of Book 1, its authority – the impeccable sources.

- Decent scipt - always more going on than it appear.

- Everything has to arise from a character

- Weakest scenarios where there a plot but no characters.

Conclusion

In this chapter, we have looked at some of the ways of creating a voice, ways that have involved transforming 'real life' into something more arresting, something that contributes to the power of story. At every step, you will notice that writing is about more than invention: more properly, it is about adapting and transforming the real world, so that a reader or audience reflects on that very same real world. At the heart of each act of creation is the process of editing. In the next chapter, you will be looking at more unusual voices, voices that are found in poems and in particular kinds of prose, and you will be attempting to create more surprising voices than those you have encountered so far.

References

Allen, W. and Brickman, M. (2000 [1982]) *Annie Hall*, London, Faber and Faber.

Churchill, C. (1990 [1980]) *Three More Sleepless Nights* in *Shorts*, London, Nick Hern Books.

Davis, R. (2008) *Writing Dialogue for Scripts*, London, A & C Black.

De-Lovely (2004) film, directed by Irwin Winkler, written by Jay Cocks, USA, MGM.

Esslin, M. (1963) 'Godot and his children' in Armstrong, W. (ed.) *Experimental Drama*, London, Bell.

Fitzgerald, S. (1925) *The Great Gatsby*, New York, Scribner.

Kane, L. (ed.) (2001) *David Mamet in Conversation*, Ann Arbor, MI, University of Michigan Press.

MacShane, F. (1986 [1976]) *The Life of Raymond Chandler*, London, Cape.

Mamet, D. (1993) *Oleanna*, London, Methuen Drama.

McInnes, G. (1986 [1966]) *Humping My Bluey*, London, The Hogarth Press.

Nixon, R.M. and Haldeman, H.R. (1999–2002 [1972]) 'Transcript of a recording of a meeting between the President and H.R. Haldeman in the Oval Office on June 23, 1972 from 10:04 to 11:39 am' [online] in Goldman, J. (ed.) *History and Politics Out Loud*, Evanston, IL, Northwestern University; an audio file of this transcript is also available online, http://www.hpol.org/transcript.php?id=92 (accessed 20 July 2010).

Pierrepoint (2005) film, directed by Adrian Shergold, written by Bob Mills and Jeff Pope, UK, Granada Television.

Pinter, H. (1977 [1960]) *The Caretaker*, London, Eyre Methuen.

Pinter, H. (1991) *Plays: One*, London, Methuen.

Ralph, P. (2008) *Deep Cut*, London, Oberon Books.

Robison, M. (1992 [1977]) 'Pretty Ice' in Ford, R. (ed.) *The Granta Book of the American Short Story*, vol. 1, London, Granta Books, pp. 434–9.

Seger, L. (1990) *Creating Unforgettable Characters*, New York, Holt Paperbacks.

Stein, S. (2003 [1995]) *Solutions for Writers: Practical Craft Techniques for Fiction and Non-fiction*, London, Souvenir Press.

Wells, H.G. (1972 [1909]) *Tono-Bungay*, London, Pan.

Further reading

Brande, D. (1981 [1934]) *Becoming a Writer*, New York, Harcourt, Brace.

Cox, A. (2005) *Writing Short Stories*, Oxford, Routledge.

Readings

Reading 3.1: 'Pretty Ice'

I was up the whole night before my fiancé was due to arrive from the East – drinking coffee, restless and pacing, my ears ringing. When the television signed off, I sat down with a packet of the month's bills and figured amounts on a lined tally sheet in my checkbook. Under the spray of a high-intensity lamp, my left hand moved rapidly over the touch tablets of my calculator.

Will, my fiancé, was coming from Boston on the six-fifty train – the dawn train, the only train that still stopped in the small Ohio city where I lived. At six-fifteen I was still at my accounts; I was getting some pleasure from transcribing the squarish green figures that appeared in the window of my calculator. 'Schwab Dental Clinic,' I printed in a raveled backhand. 'Thirty-eight and 50/100.'

A car horn interrupted me. I looked over my desktop and out the living-room window of my rented house. The saplings in my little yard were encased in ice. There had been snow all week, and then an ice storm. In the glimmering driveway in front of my garage, my mother was peering out of her car. I got up and turned off my lamp and capped my ivory Mont Blanc pen. I found a coat in the semidark in the hall, and wound a knitted muffler at my throat. Crossing the living room, I looked away from the big pine mirror; I didn't want to see how my face and hair looked after a night of accounting.

My yard was a frozen pond, and I was careful on the walkway. My mother hit her horn again. Frozen slush came through the toe of one of my chukka boots, and I stopped on the path and frowned at her. I could see her breath rolling away in clouds from the cranked-down window of her Mazda. I have never owned a car nor learned to drive, but I had a low opinion of my mother's compact. My father and I used to enjoy big cars, with tops that came down. We were both tall and we wanted what he called 'stretch room.' My father had been dead for fourteen years, but I resented my mother's buying a car in which he would not have fitted.

'Now what's wrong? Are you coming?' my mother said.

'Nothing's wrong except that my shoes are opening around the soles,' I said. 'I just paid a lot of money for them.'

I got in on the passenger side. The car smelled of wet wool and Mother's hair spray. Someone had done her hair with a minty-white rinse, and the hair was held in place by a zebra-striped headband.

'I think you're getting a flat,' I said. 'That retread you bought for the left front is going.'

She backed the car out of the drive, using the rear-view mirror. 'I finally got a boy I can trust, at the Exxon station,' she said. 'He said that tire will last until hot weather.'

Out on the street, she accelerated too quickly and the rear of the car swung left. The tires whined for an instant on the old snow and then caught. We were knocked back in our seats a little, and an empty Kleenex box slipped off the dash and onto the floor carpet.

'This is going to be something,' my mother said. 'Will sure picked an awful day to come.'

My mother had never met him. My courtship with Will had all happened in Boston. I was getting my doctorate there, in musicology. Will was involved with his research at Boston U., and with teaching botany to undergraduates. 'You're sure he'll be at the station?' my mother said. 'Can the trains go in this weather? I don't see how they do.'

'I talked to him on the phone yesterday. He's coming.'

'How did he sound?' my mother said.

To my annoyance, she begun to hum to herself.

I said, 'He's had rotten news about his work. Terrible, in fact.'

'Explain his work to me again,' she said.

'He's a plant taxonomist.'

'Yes?' my mother said. 'What does that mean?'

'It means he doesn't have a lot of money,' I said. 'He studies grasses. He said on the phone he's been turned down for a research grant that would have meant a great deal to us. Apparently the work he's been doing for the past seven or so years is irrelevant or outmoded. I guess "superficial" is what he told me.'

'I won't mention it to him, then,' my mother said.

We came to the expressway. Mother steered the car through some small windblown snow dunes and down the entrance ramp. She followed two yellow salt trucks with winking blue beacons that were moving side by side down the center and right-hand lanes.

'I think losing the grant means we should postpone the wedding,' I said. 'I want Will to have his bearings before I step into his life for good.'

'Don't wait too much longer, though,' my mother said.

After a couple of miles, she swung off the expressway. We went past some tall high-tension towers with connecting cables that looked like staff lines on a sheet of music. We were in the decaying neighborhood near the tracks. 'Now I know this is right,' Mother said. 'There's our old sign.'

The sign was a tall billboard, black and white, that advertised my father's dance studio. The studio had been closed for years and the building it had been in was gone. The sign showed a man in a tuxedo waltzing with a woman in an evening gown. I was always sure it was a waltz. The dancers were nearly two stories high, and the weather had bleached them into phantoms. The lettering – the name of the studio, my father's name – had disappeared.

'They've changed everything,' my mother said, peering about. 'Can this be the station?'

We went up a little drive that wound past a cindery lot full of flatbed trucks and that ended up at the smudgy brownstone depot.

'Is that your Will?' Mother said.

Will was on the station platform, leaning against a baggage truck. He had a duffle bag between his shoes and a plastic cup of coffee in his mittened hand. He seemed to have put on weight, girlishly, through the hips, and his face looked thicker to me, from temple to temple. His gold-rimmed spectacles looked too small.

My mother stopped in an empty cab lane, and I got out and called to Will. It wasn't far from the platform to the car, and Will's pack wasn't a large one, but he seemed to be winded when he got to me. I let him kiss me, and then he stepped back and blew a cold breath and drank from the coffee cup, with his eyes on my face.

Mother was pretending to be busy with something in her handbag, not paying attention to me and Will.

'I look awful,' I said.

'No, no, but I probably do,' Will said. 'No sleep, and I'm fat. So this is your town?'

He tossed the coffee cup at an oil drum and glanced around at the cold train yards and low buildings. A brass foundry was throwing a yellowish column of smoke over a line of Canadian Pacific boxcars.

I said, 'The problem is you're looking at the wrong side of the tracks.'

A wind whipped Will's lank hair across his face. 'Does your mom smoke?' he said. 'I ran out in the middle of the night on the train, and the club car was closed. Eight hours across Pennsylvania without a cigarette.'

The car horn sounded as my mother climbed from behind the wheel. 'That was an accident,' she said, because I was frowning at her. 'Hello. Are you Will?' She came around the car and stood on tiptoes and kissed him. 'You picked a miserable day to come and visit us.'

She was using her young-girl voice, and I was embarrassed for her. 'He needs a cigarette,' I said.

Will got into the back of the car and I sat beside my mother again. After we started up, Mother said, 'Why doesn't Will stay at my place, in your old room, Belle? I'm all alone there, with plenty of space to kick around in.'

'We'll be able to get him a good motel,' I said quickly, before Will could answer. 'Let's try that Ramada, over near the new elementary school.' It was odd, after he had come all the way from Cambridge, but I didn't want him in my old room, in the house where I had been a child. 'I'd put you at my place,' I said, 'but there's mountains of tax stuff all over.'

'You've been busy,' he said.

'Yes,' I said. I sat sidewise, looking at each of them in turn. Will had some blackish spots around his mouth – ballpoint ink, maybe. I wished he had freshened up and put on a better shirt before leaving the train.

'It's up to you two, then,' my mother said.

I could tell she was disappointed in Will. I don't know what she expected. I was thirty-one when I met him. I had probably dated fewer men in my life than she had gone out with in a single year at her sorority. She had always been successful with men.

'William was my late husband's name,' my mother said. 'Did Belle ever tell you?'

'No,' Will said. He was smoking one of Mother's cigarettes.

'I always like the name,' she said. 'Did you know we ran a dance studio?'

I groaned.

'Oh, let me brag if I want to,' my mother said. 'He was such a handsome man.'

It was true. They were both handsome – mannequins, a pair of dolls who had spent half their lives in evening clothes. But my father had looked old in the end, in a business in which you had to stay young. He had trouble with his eyes, which were bruised-looking and watery, and he had to wear glasses with thick lenses.

I said, 'It was in the dance studio that my father ended his life, you know. In the ballroom.'

'You told me,' Will said, at the same instant my mother said, 'Don't talk about it.'

My father killed himself with a service revolver. We never found out where he had bought it, or when. He was found in his warm-up clothes – a pullover sweater and pleated pants. He was wearing his tap shoes, and he had a short towel folded around his neck. He had aimed the gun barrel down his mouth, so the bullet would not shatter the wall of mirrors behind him. I was twenty then – old enough to find out how he did it.

My mother had made a wrong turn and we were on Buttles Avenue. 'Go there,' I said, pointing down a street beside Garfield Park. We passed a group of paper boys who were riding bikes with saddlebags. They were going slow, because of the ice.

'Are you very discouraged, Will?' my mother said. 'Belle tells me you are having a run of bad luck.'

'You could say so,' Will said. 'A little rough water.'

'I'm sorry,' Mother said. 'What seems to be the trouble?'

Will said, 'Well, this will be oversimplifying, but essentially what I do is take a weed and evaluate its structure and growth and habitat, and so forth.'

'What's wrong with that?' my mother said.

'Nothing. But it isn't enough.'

'I get it,' my mother said uncertainly.

I had taken a mirror and a comb from my handbag and I was trying for a clean center-part in my hair. I was thinking about finishing my bill paying.

Will said, 'What do you want to do after I check in, Belle? What about breakfast?'

'I've got to go home for a while and clean up that tax jazz, or I'll never rest,' I said. 'I'll just show up at your motel later. If we ever find it.'

'That'll be fine,' Will said.

Mother said, 'I'd offer to serve you two dinner tonight, but I think you'll want to leave me out of it. I know how your father and I felt after he went away sometimes. Which way do I turn here?'

We had stopped at an intersection near the iron gates of the park. Behind the gates there was a frozen pond, where a single early morning skater was skating backward, expertly crossing his blades.

I couldn't drive a car but, like my father, I have always enjoyed maps and atlases. During automobile trips, I liked comparing distances on maps. I liked the words *latitude*, *cartography*, *meridian*. It was extremely annoying to me that Mother had gotten us turned around and lost in our own city, and I was angry with Will all of a sudden, for wasting seven years on something superficial.

'What about up that way?' Will said to my mother, pointing to the left. 'There's some traffic up by that light, at least.'

I leaned forward in my seat and started combing my hair all over again.

'There's no hurry,' my mother said.

'How do you mean?' I asked her.

'To get William to the motel,' she said. 'I know everybody complains, but I think an ice storm is a beautiful thing. Let's enjoy it.'

She waved her cigarette at the windshield. The sun had burnt through and was gleaming in the branches of all the maples and buckeye trees in the park. 'It's twinkling like a stage set,' Mother said.

'It is pretty,' I said.

Will said, 'It'll make a bad-looking spring. A lot of shrubs get damaged and turn brown, and the trees don't blossom right.'

For once I agreed with my mother. Everything was quiet and holding still. Everything was in place, the way it was supposed to be. I put my comb away and smiled back at Will – because I knew it was for the last time.

Source: Robison, M. (1992 [1977]) 'Pretty Ice' in Ford, R. (ed.) *The Granta Book of the American Short Story*, vol. 1, London, Granta Books, pp. 434–9.

Reading 3.2: from *Humping My Bluey*

Barton's sister Lindsay, a severe girl with gold braids, and her friend who has brown hair and a slightly supercilious expression, are setting up a ping-pong net on the dining table. Lindsay is in a difficult mood. We don't seem to see eye to eye on whether you should bat from beneath the table or whether it's all right to do a spin serve on the sandpapered side of the bat from *above* the table. While we are arguing in a pointless, well-I'm-sure-I-don't-care-it-couldn't-mean-less-to-me manner, Barton and the friend have disappeared. Lindsay and I are stuck with each other.

'Why do you do your hair in pigtails, Lindsay?'

'Don't call them pigtails. It's rude.'

'What do you want me to call them?'

'I don't particularly want you to call them anything; but if you must mention them, they're plaits.'

'O.K., plaits then. Why do you do your hair in plaits?'

'Because I like them. What business is it of yours?'

'It makes you look like a little girl.'

'Well that's suitable for a little boy isn't it?'

'Don't get sore at me.'

'Then don't make personal remarks. There's the door-bell.'

'That's just an excuse not to talk to me.'

'No, it really is the bell. Excuse *me*.'

Source: McInnes, G. (1986 [1966]) *Humping My Bluey*, London, The Hogarth Press, p. 30.

Reading 3.3: from *Writing Dialogue for Scripts*

	JILL, CHERRY, PENNY and SHEILA *face the audience.*
JILL	The front window, the windscreen, it came out in one piece – I suppose it's meant to do that, and we all crawled out of that.
	JILL, CHERRY, PENNY and SHEILA *take up positions as though in a car.* JILL *is driving,* CHERRY *has her head out of the window and* SHEILA *and* PENNY *are in the back. They are all obviously enjoying themselves.*
SHEILA	(*yell – as though over the sound of the engine*) We –
PENNY	(*yell*) – were –
SHEILA	(*yell*) – going –
JILL	Like the clappers!
PENNY	– in this beaten-up old thing.
JILL	I don't think it had ever done this speed in its life before, and Cherry –
CHERRY	Yoohoo!!
JILL	– had got her head out the window.
PENNY	(*to* JILL) Is this all it can do?
SHEILA	(*to* JILL) Put your foot down!
JILL	It's flat on the floor as it is!
CHERRY	We're *going* to get there before it starts!

SHEILA	And it was fun.
JILL	It felt great!
PENNY	All of us together!
	All freeze. This is held for a few moments, and then while the others stay frozen, JILL *turns to us.*
JILL	I don't remember any screaming, though there may have been. Someone may have said 'Oh God.'
	A tyre'd blown.
	We just sort of clung on.
	PENNY *and* SHEILA *slowly turn to us, but* CHERRY *remains frozen.*
PENNY	Sort of clung on …
SHEILA	Clung onto …
JILL	Clung onto whatever.
	Now suddenly all, including CHERRY, *are totally unfrozen, and screaming, as together they turn over and over.*
	All lie still, silent.
JILL	And I thought, 'I'm still alive. I'm still here.'
	(slight pause)
	You there?
PENNY	Yeah.
SHEILA	Yeah.
	(slight pause)
JILL	Cherry?
	(slight pause)
JILL	Cherry was still there, God knows how.
CHERRY	I was in hospital for three months, traction, on my back. But I was alive.

Source: Davis, R. (2008) *Writing Dialogue for Scripts*, London, A & C Black, pp. 188–9.

4   Poetic voices

Bill Greenwell

Contents

Aims

This chapter will:

- further develop your understanding of the invented voice by exploring the art and artifice of 'poetic' language
- give you an insight into the way poetry relies on patterns of sound
- give you the experience of trying out brief exercises in creating poetry
- help you to understand the way creative writers use a variety of strategies and forms to create distinctive voices in their texts.

Materials you will need

- DVD 2 (audio and video)

Introduction

In the last chapter, you looked at the art and artifice of using voices in writing, and the relationship those voices had with 'real life'. In this chapter you will be looking at how to create a 'poetic' voice, and how to create a poem.

Poetic

- Prose
- rhyming
- flavey

Poem

- verses, stanzas
- Pace
- Rhythm
- rhyme

4.1   The meaning of 'poetic'

The difference between the voices and texts in the last chapter and the ones you will encounter and invent in this chapter is that in this chapter the voices are consciously 'unreal', which is to say that they are seeking to go, self-consciously, beyond the mimicry of real-life voices. But first, it's best that we define our terms.

Activity

1   First, spend five to ten minutes writing down what you understand by the words 'poetic' and 'poem'. Do the two words mean the same thing?

2   Now read the three extracts in Reading 4.1. All three are experimental prose. How might they be said to be 'poetic'?

This activity should take you about 25 minutes.

Discussion

1   'Poetic' can mean, simply, that language is written in poetic form, and it is on this sense of 'poetic' that this chapter will mainly concentrate. The word 'poetic' can also be used as a compliment, almost as a synonym for 'moving' – this is the sense in which Lynda Prescott used it in Chapter 4 of Book 1, when describing a speech towards the end of *The Island* (Section 4.2). It can mean 'using language creatively' – the sense in which David Mamet uses it in Chapter 3 of this book (Section 3.2). However, 'poetic' can also be used to suggest a rich, perhaps even elaborate language, one that depends much more than everyday speech on overt **metaphor** and **simile**. By implication there is something self-conscious about this kind of 'poetic' voice, which is by no means confined to poetry. There are many examples of prose writers and dramatists who use a rich, intense vocabulary, or who write in a way that celebrates language as art almost more than as communication.

2   The three extracts in Reading 4.1 are taken respectively from a short prose fiction by Samuel Beckett (1906–89), a radio play by Dylan Thomas (1914–53) and a stage play by Bryony Lavery (b. 1947). Each uses language in a way that might be called unusual, perhaps eccentric, and in a more intense way than we would associate with more conventional prose. The writing is consciously straining at the boundaries of what is expected – either by coining words, or by running words together or punctuating (with commas in Beckett's case, and with line breaks in Lavery's case) in an unusual manner. There is in each case a heightened sense of language as something more mobile and fluent than we might find in everyday conversation.

The voices in the three extracts are super-distinctive. In a note to another play, *A Wedding Story* (2007 [2000]), Lavery is explicit about her unusual use of language:

> This play is laid out to help the actors find
> the true rhythms of dramatic speech.
>
> None of the characters speak in sentences
> or observe punctuation or breathe at the right time.
>
> Because   often
> They are in   torment.
>
> The short lines, the spaces within or between lines,
> are there on purpose to indicate the subtext and
> to help the performer to find the physical
> and emotional journey within a speech.
>
> I hope the reader will observe the deliberate
> eccentricities of my punctuation …
>
> (Lavery, 2007 [2000], p. 6)

In defining 'poem' in the previous activity, you may have written something about its shape or layout. If you open any book of poetry, the first thing you will see is that the lines have been arranged in some way. You will see more white space on the page than is usual for a page of prose fiction, and you will sense that there is some structure or form. You may see the poem laid out in **stanzas**, you may see the poem set out in lines of roughly similar length or you may see the poem experimenting with lines of different length. It is hard to imagine a poem that does not look like a poem. However, this won't do as a definition, since you could easily rearrange a passage of prose to resemble a poem.

What you will not see straightaway, unless the poem is using a traditional rhyme scheme, is the importance to a poem of repetition. Rhyme itself, incidentally, comes in many forms, and some of them are not instantly visible. The box on rhyme explains the many ways in which the word 'rhyme' can be applied.

Rhyme

There are many different forms of rhyme, of which the most well known is end-rhyme, which (as the term suggests) occurs at the end of the line. An exact rhyme (e.g. 'bend'/'send' or 'wind'/'pinned' is called 'full rhyme'. As you saw in Book 1, a rhyme scheme can be described using upper case letters, e.g. ABCB would mean that the second line rhymed with the fourth, and that the other two lines did not rhyme.

Rhyme scheme was explained in relation to the Donne poetry you studied in Chapter 2 of Book 1 (Section 2.1).

Half-rhyme, sometimes called 'slant rhyme', is when the end-words are approximately the same – most often the consonants are the same, but the vowel between them is varied: so for instance 'main'/'mean', 'filling'/'falling' are half-rhymes. Half-rhyme can be put to two good uses: the inexactness of the rhyme can help create a mood of dissonance, of uncertainty. Half-rhymes can also quieten a poem: exact rhymes can make a poem more assertive, while half-rhymes can be used to tone down that directness.

Near-rhyme is when the final words are similar, so that there is the suggestion of rhyme, no more – as when a stanza in the poem 'Considering the Snail' by Thom Gunn (1929–2004) uses the end-words 'stirring', 'tell', 'there', 'nothing', 'all', 'later' (Gunn, 2007, p. 20). This kind of almost invisible rhyming can give a poem a surprising sense of structure.

You can hear Gunn read his poem online at *The Poetry Archive* (Gunn, 2005–2010).

Internal rhyme is when words within one line, or in one line and in another, or in one line and at the end of another, match each other as full end-rhyme does, as in 'Hometown' by Carol Ann Duffy (b. 1955):

> What am I wearing as I pine for the future
> alone, down by the river by the Brine Baths
> longing to get out? But I only threw a stone …

> (Duffy, 1991, p. 10)

Just as there can be full internal rhyme, there can also be half-rhyme buried in a line, or a sequence of similar sounds, particularly vowel sounds. Consonantal echoes can make a poem too obvious, and need to be used sparingly.

4.2   Repetition and poetry

When you create a poem, you are consciously shaping language, more consciously, I would argue, than if you are shaping any prose, even the experimentally 'poetic' prose in Reading 4.1. And the most important method used by poets to shape language is repetition.

There are three particular ways in which the writing of poetry can use repetition. One is the repetition of some formal aspect of structure, such as the use of a pattern of stanzas (sometimes called '**verses**', although 'verse' is more commonly now used to define a section of a song). Another is the repetition, either exactly or less precisely, of a phrase. A third and perhaps most important device is the repetition of sounds – either of vowels or of consonants – which may happen across the length of a poem or at specific intervals. The repetition of sounds is affected by where the beat of a line falls – if the beat falls on similar sounds, it is more noticeable. So, for instance, in the Michael Longley poem 'War & Peace' (see Book 1, Chapter 3, Reading 3.4), the beat falls in the following line on two short *u* sounds ('*o*ther'/'r*u*nning') and two long *o* sounds ('c*o*ld'/'sn*o*w'):

The other running cold as hailstones, snow water.

Of course, poets do not write by thinking up sound-patterns and then grafting subjects on to them. However, in successive drafts of poems, the kinds of amendments that poets make are frequently to do with adjusting the pattern of sound and other repetitions so that they are appropriate. So it is a good idea to be clear about the ways in which vowels and consonants, syllables and stresses, and different kinds of rhyme might work. You might find this quite 'technical', but my approach here is to give you some of the detail about the way sound works, before approaching the idea of creating poems. Many people are anxious about creating poems, but having a sense of their mechanics should help demystify the process.

Vowels

The vowels in English are *a, e, i, o, u*, and sometimes also *y* (which is a consonant or vowel depending on its context). They are the sounds made by breath through the larynx and mouth that do not

---

use the tongue, lips or teeth. As noted in Chapter 1 of this book, the relationship between the alphabet and speech sounds is not straightforward, and so sociolinguists will use a specialised alphabet such as the IPA when they wish to describe speech in a detailed and accurate way. What I am giving you here, though, is more a lay guide to speech sounds, which is sufficient for our present purposes.

Vowels can be either long or short, and spelling alone will not show this. A short vowel sound would include:

a   as in 'c*a*n'

e   as in 'b*e*d'

i   as in 't*i*n'

o   as in 'h*o*t'

u   as in 'cr*u*mb'

y   as in 'p*y*ramid' or 'hand*y*' (note the difference).

A long vowel sound would include:

a   as in 'f*a*te'

e   as in 'sw*e*de'

i   as in 't*i*me'

o   as in h*o*tel'

u   as in 'fl*u*te' or 'd*u*ty' (note the difference)

y   as in 'wh*y*'.

However, there are many other ways of combining vowels to create a longer sound – '*aa*rdvark', 'b*ee*t', 'w*oo*l', 'sp*oo*l', 'C*ae*sar', 'w*ei*ght', 'bel*ie*ve', 'w*ai*f', 'g*ao*l', 'c*au*l', 'T*eu*tonic', 'f*oa*l', 'sp*oi*l', 'm*ou*th', 'f*ou*r', 't*ou*gh', 't*ui*le', 'b*eau*tiful'. These vowel sounds correspond to items in the list above. However, there are many instances of vowels that are changed by the (usually silent, depending on your dialect) consonant succeeding them: 'h*a*rd', 'b*i*rth', 'h*ea*rth', 'sp*u*r', and so on.

The repetition of a vowel sound is called assonance.

Consonants

The English alphabet gives us twenty-one consonants, including *y*. However, some of the alphabetical sounds are duplicates, as with the 'soft' *c* of 'dice' and the 'hard' *c* of 'biscuit', which are respectively duplicated by *s* and *k*. And there are sounds simply not represented in the alphabet, including both 'hard' and 'soft' versions of *th* (as in 'this' and 'youth'), each of which had separate symbols in Old English. Many consonants are no longer sounded, as with the *k* in 'knot', and there are subtle other differences, such as the sound of *g* after an *n*, as in 'sing' and 'longer'.

There are of course many combinations of consonants – if you take a common word such as 'strength', there are six successive consonantal sounds (*s, t, r, n, g, th*). That means the word takes longer to say than a word with fewer consonants, or to 'hear' when reading. That will slow a line down. Writers do not sit and count consonants – but it is a good idea to be aware of their potential effect. Some consonants are also invariably 'hard' and others 'soft', but this does depend on frequency and context. Certainly the consonantal sounds *d, k, t* are harder, just as the consonantal sounds *f, l, m, r* and *s* are generally softer. There is a particular word for the repetition of an *s* sound – sibilance.

Consonants can thin or thicken a line, causing it to accelerate or decelerate, just as they can make it more or less aggressive, or more or less gentle in sound.

The repetition of a consonantal sound is called alliteration.

Activity

This activity should take you about 30 minutes.

Before you tackle the main part of this activity, read the boxes on vowels and consonants as many times as you need to, to absorb the information fully before moving on to the second part of the activity. You may find it helpful to read aloud the words given as examples.

I'm now going to ask you to experiment. What you write does not have to make perfect sense. You can even see the activity as an exercise in pure sound. Below is an opening phrase. I want you to create a pair of lines continuing from the phrase, in which there is some form of repetition, either of a vowel or consonant – as much repetition as you like. You can rhyme the pair of lines if you like, but it's not necessary.

It's time to catch ... *another mouse*
We're sure has ending i the house

Discussion

It would have been fine if your lines were nonsensical, perhaps as follows:

> It's time to catch the accidental patch, to climb
> the hat-stand while the crimes are watched and tied.

Or you might quite reasonably have made sense with your lines, as in:

> It's time to catch a final glimpse of you,
> and naturally I'm trying to keep track.

I am not suggesting that this kind of forced patterning will lead you easily to a poem. It is a limbering-up exercise, and what I have been trying to do here is to concentrate almost entirely on echoing the *ti-*, or *t* or *-ime* sounds in 'time', and the *-at/-atch* sound in 'catch'. In the nonsense version, it is of course easier: 'time'/'climb'/'crimes'/'tied' and 'catch'/'patch'/'hat'/'watch'. (Notice that 'watch' is a half-rhyme.) In the second attempt, I have 'time'/'final'/'I'm'/'track', and 'catch'/'nat-'/'track'. I have included 'track' twice because it echoes the *t* of 'time' and the short *a* of 'catch'.

In the previous activity, rather artificially, I have constructed a brief pattern of repetitions, which we might call 'harmonies'. In the next section, I will look at how a song lyric and a poem use echoes like this to construct their poetic voices.

4.3   Song and poem

Poetry is a lineal descendant of song. In a pre-literate age, a song would need to have possessed the essential qualities required for being committed to memory – that is, a great deal of repetition, including the use of refrains. (Homer's *Iliad*, referred to in Chapter 3 of Book 1, is full of repetitions.) The Welsh word *cerdd* means both 'song' *and* 'poem', and 'sonnet' comes from the Italian word for 'little song', *sonetto*.

Songs continue to be repetitive, to use (for instance) choruses, as you can hear from the examples given by Fiona Richards in Chapter 2 of Book 1. Poetry has developed from being spoken to being written (although, of course, poems continue to be read aloud, to be recited or performed). As they have developed, the repetitions and echoes they use have become more subtle. In contemporary poetry – much of which continues to use rhyme – the repetitions that give the poem its voice are more deeply buried in the text. What gives a poem its distinctive flavour is often its repetition not just of words but of sounds, in particular the sounds of vowels. In effect, poems become like echo-chambers.

On DVD 2 you can find a recording of Joni Mitchell's song 'Amelia' and hear Jane Draycott reading her poem 'Golf'.

In the next activity you will look at two readings, both of which explore a sense of separation. One of them is the opening of a relatively contemporary song, 'Amelia' by Joni Mitchell (b. 1943), and the other is a contemporary poem, 'Golf' by Jane Draycott (b. 1954). Mitchell's song is addressed to Amelia Earhart, the adventurous airwoman of the 1920s and 1930s, with whom the voice identifies. Draycott's poem opens with the idea of golfers being always 'one step ahead', and develops the idea into a deeper sense of the separation between one group of people and another, into perhaps the separation between the present and the past.

This activity should take you about 20 minutes.

Activity

Turn to Readings 4.2 and 4.3, and read Mitchell's song 'Amelia' and Draycott's poem 'Golf'. What repetitions and echoes can you find in each?

Discussion

The repetitions in Mitchell's song are predictably more obvious – *because* it is a song. There is a refrain ('Amelia, it was just a false alarm'); there are several examples of rhyme or near-rhyme: 'planes'/ 'terrain', 'guitar'/'alarm', 'blue'/'you', 'charms'/'alarm'. There are also several internal echoes: 'across'/'spotted', 'vapor trails', 'fly'/'wild'/'time', 'hexagram'/'heavens', 'drone'/'so', 'engines'/'seasons', 'through'/'you'. And a key phrase is repeated too: 'It was'/'it was'/'it was'/'it was'/'it was'. Not only that, the words 'Amelia' and 'alarm' both use the same two key consonants, *m* and *l*. And an interesting echo, which you will hear on the DVD, 'false'/'alarm', comes from Mitchell's Canadian pronunciation, and is an example of the regional variation referred to by Philip Seargeant in Chapter 1 of this book.

The repetitions in 'Amelia' not only make the song easier to remember, but also to sing. In Draycott's poem, however, there are just as many repetitions and echoes, less obvious at first, and principally of vowel-sounds: 'figures'/'kings', 'type'/'migrant', 'adventurous'/'step'/'ahead', 'simply'/'instinct', 'oasis'/'gaze', 'well'/'felt', 'boundless'/'bare', 'bare'/'somewhere', 'elsewhere'/'ahead', 'struck'/'clock', 'again'/'blame', 'us'/'gulf'. There are repetitions, too, of words: 'first to'/'first then to', 'strike'/'struck'/'struck', 'ahead'/'ahead', 'again'/'again'. She also half-rhymes the title with the final word.

To put it another way, the pattern of harmonies in Draycott's poem is more intricate than in Mitchell's song, although both of them have patterns of echo and repetition. Draycott's poem has also cunningly borrowed the phrase 'boundless and bare' from Percy Bysshe Shelley's 'Ozymandias' (1818), a poem set in a desert, and about a confrontation between a bewildered onlooker and a wrecked and ancient memorial plinth: emphasising the distance between present and past.

What creates the poetic voice – what marks it out – is the attention to what we might call the melody of words. This is not to suggest that a writer obsesses over every echo – sometimes echoes occur naturally in the writing, in the discovery of the subject and mood. But the drafting process in each case will have woven the echoes in more securely. Nor is it to suggest that every song or poem contains such a proliferation of echoes and repetitions. But it is to underline the way in which a poetic voice distinguishes itself from the everyday voice by the use of such devices.

You can hear a fuller discussion of 'Golf', and Jane Draycott's discussion of drafting a poem in 'Interview with Jane Draycott' on DVD 2.

4.4   Syllables and stress

You may be familiar with some of the technical terms used to describe the patterns of lines in metric poetry (for instance 'iambic pentameter'). There are many technical terms, but they can be baffling if you are attempting to compose poetry.

It is important, however, to know the difference between a stressed syllable and an unstressed syllable, because a writer uses the syllables on which the beat or stress falls to create both rhythmic and harmonic patterns. Although there are some slight regional variations, the stress pattern of any word is quite easy to work out. The word 'father' is pronounced with the stress on the first syllable – *fath*er. The word 'across' is pronounced with the stress on the second syllable – a*cross*. The word 'frightening' has a stress on the first syllable – *fright*ening. Sometimes the strength of the stress on a syllable can be affected by the place it occupies in a line: you can only really work this out by reading it aloud.

So, for instance, in the poem 'My father carries me across a field' by George Szirtes (b. 1948), the opening lines are:

> My father carries me across a field.
> It's night and there are trenches filled with snow.
> Thick mud. We're careful to remain concealed
>
> From something frightening I don't yet know.

(Szirtes, 2004, p. 57)

(The space between the third and fourth lines indicates a break between two three-line stanzas.) I would say that the stresses fall, perhaps with slightly different weight, on the emboldened syllables below:

> My *fath*er *carr*ies me a*cross* a *field*.
> It's *night* and there are *trench*es *filled* with *snow*.
> *Thick* *mud*. We're *care*ful to re*main* con*cealed*
>
> From *some*thing *fright*ening I *don't* yet *know*.

In the last line, perhaps that might be *don't yet know* (i.e. beat, beat, beat).

Even if locating the pattern of stress is sometimes a slightly inexact art, developing a sense of the rise and fall, and an idea of the pattern of emphatic and weaker syllables, is important for the creator of a poetic voice. Poetry is more musical than most prose – because, as I've noted, its ancestry is in song or in chant. Aristotle wrote in his *Poetics* (1996, p.7) of 'melody and rhythm' being 'natural' to humans, and poetry makes the most of that tendency.

4.5 Writing in a poetic voice

Starting to write a poem can seem a daunting prospect. To begin with, however, you are only going to try some limbering-up exercises, and what you write may well seem rough and ready. That is an important part of the process, however. Nearly all the poems you have read will have started from a few jotted notes of observation, or a phrase the writer has overheard, or a very vague idea. It is important, however, that you focus on using contemporary language, and stay away from the many archaisms that spring to mind when thinking about poems you may have come across, and enjoyed, and even remembered well enough to quote. Here are some examples of the kind of word I'm thinking of:

old fashioned

> wondrous, drear, bedecked, 'tis, mead, yonder, pent, mourn, naught, musing, adorn, vale, wilt, shalt, thou, thee, citadel, aplenty, woe, wrought, forlorn, saith, brow, avail, wherefore, o'er.

It is difficult to be prescriptive – in the right context, 'mourn' might be appropriate, for instance – but avoid words that you would not hear in everyday conversation, for which there are good alternatives. The words cited above are the kind frequently used in Victorian hymns. This doesn't mean you can't raid the dictionary: there are some words just itching to be rescued and reused. The words to edit out of your poetic vocabulary are those that sound as if they've been borrowed from poems written a hundred or more years ago.

A noun that denotes an idea, emotion, feeling, quality or other abstract or intangible concept

Equally, it's a good idea to stick to natural word order. You wouldn't hear anyone say 'To the shops shall I go'. They'd more probably say 'I'm off to the shops'. When you invert the natural order of words, especially if you do it to make a rhyme fit, the result generally sounds clunky. Two other suggestions at this stage are to avoid abstract nouns (e.g. obedience, love, hate, desire, anxiety), choosing instead to show the mood or quality you are describing, and to stay away from clusters of multisyllabic words. The power of a contemporary poetic voice comes from its skill with sound, structure, image and idea – and also from its being creative but unforced, especially in its rhythm.

Activity

Create a list of twenty words with a long *a* sound in them in which the weight of the pronunciation falls on that syllable. A long *a* sound is as in 'gale', 'ageing', 'defame', 'we*i*ght', 'betr*a*yal', 'pass*é*', 'fa*i*ling', 'faded', 'constra*i*nt', 'cradle'. Notice that the spelling of the long *a* sound can vary. In the examples given here, it is on the *a* sound that the beat falls; other words may also have a long *a* sound, for example 'amoral', 'régime' and 'portrait', but in these words the weight falls on *-mor*, *-gime* and *port-* respectively. Choose eight of these twenty words.

Now look at Figure 4.1 and write eight single-sentence statements from the point of view of the person pictured in it, each one of which contains one or more of the words you have selected. The statements do not have to start with the word 'I'. Also, although the painting is Victorian, the language you use should be contemporary.

This activity should take you about 30 minutes.

- rage
- ~~dilemma~~
- elated
- lose
- portrayed
- tidy
- doom
- loom
- ~~undo~~
- feeder
- reader

Figure 4.1   Sir John Everett Millais, *Mariana in the Moated Grange*, 1851, oil on panel, 60 × 50 cm. The Makins Collection. Photo: © The Makins Collection/The Bridgeman Art Library.

Discussion

You may have found that your list of statements was very peculiar, that they varied in length or that you found yourself making unconscious connections between them. For this activity, it doesn't matter. However, notice that I have been quite restrictive in what you can do. Not only have I given you a specific painting from which to work, but I have also specified a vowel sound that has to appear in each of the lines. This is because, when you are practising writing, it is usually best to operate under some constraint. If I offered you the whole of the English language and an infinite choice of images, the sheer range of possibilities would probably overwhelm you. Restricting yourself in some way creates the tension that is essential to composing words. (You have the additional constraint of the picture, too – a constraint often used in creative writing workshops, to relax writers who are worrying about choice of subject.) Here is a list of statements I've invented:

My face is as pale as a lily.

The air in here is stale and stifling.

I don't care for stained glass at all.

There is no sign of any neighbours.

It pains me to stand here like this.

I would like to complain to the management.

I'd like to get away but I don't know how to escape.

Waiting, waiting: that's all I seem to do.

For obvious reasons, this list contains a great deal of echo and some internal rhyme ('stained'/'pains'/'complain', for instance). It may be that your own list has some hidden rhymes, as well – and it will certainly have some echo, because I designed the exercise so that it would.

As it stands, its potential as a poem is spoiled by the repeated end-stopping (the eight full stops at the end of each line). To draft a coherent whole, it will almost invariably be better for the sentences to move across the lines.

Mariana

Mariana in the Moated Grange was painted by Sir John Everett Millais (1829–96) in 1851, at a time when medieval themes and images were being explored in painting by the 'Pre-Raphaelite Brotherhood' of which Millais was a founder member two years earlier. Millais had already moved away from the religious subjects favoured by some of his fellow painters, and had begun to use images from writers he admired. 'Mariana' is a poem written in 1830 by Alfred, Lord Tennyson (1809–92), and the poem is in turn based on a minor Shakespearean character rejected by her fiancé, and living alone for five years. In the Tennyson poem, she calls out 'I would that I were dead!' The figure in the painting – much admired by women at its opening – is plainly weary of her embroidery, which is not mentioned by Tennyson.

4.6 Drafting the voice

Making notes is only the first stage, and, in this case, the notes have been constrained by showing you how sound patterns might emerge. Poems about paintings or photographs are a good way of trying out voices, because they focus your imagination: the detail of what your image looks like is predetermined, although of course the choice of language you might use to describe it is open. A poem about the painting in Figure 4.1 might go in any one of dozens of different directions. These directions can't be preplanned – a poem, like a story, will find its own aim. Nonetheless, I've tried two drafts of a poem based partly on the painting and partly on my eight statements. The first one is shown in Figure 4.2. It's handwritten, although it really is a matter of preference how you write. Handwritten drafts have the advantage of allowing you to see the changes you have made more easily.

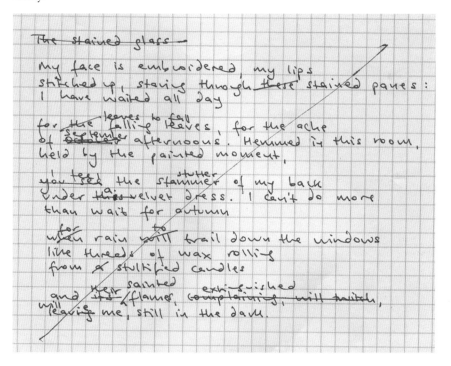

Figure 4.2   First draft of a poem based on the painting *Mariana in the Moated Grange*

You can see that I have made a sort of false start, and also that I have attempted to control the movement by using three-line stanzas (until the

final pair of lines). This was not a predetermined decision; a writer
tends to light on a structure while writing. I have now started to move
across the line-endings to give the poem more fluidity. I have also kept
the following words from my original eight lines: 'face', 'pale', 'stained',
'complain', 'wait'. I'm certainly not going to be able to use only the long
a sound in the poem: that would make it too repetitive. I have added
other echoes instead. In places I have left some choices.

By the second draft (Figure 4.3), I have made several changes.

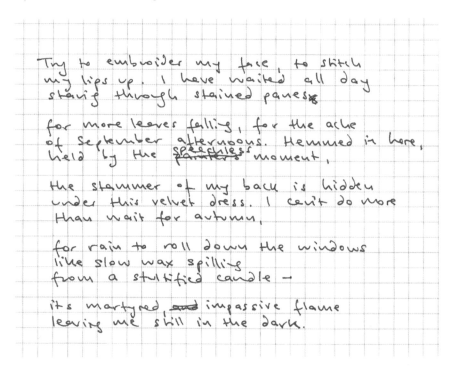

Figure 4.3   Second draft of a poem based on the painting *Mariana in the
Moated Grange*

At this stage (for this is far from a finished poem), I have focused on
the embroidery from which the woman in Millais' painting has just
stood up, and the air of frustration, of solitude, that the painting
suggests to me. The idea of waiting has led me to an image of a candle,
a candle that is not in the painting at all, and the image of the candle
has led to an image of martyrdom. In fact, if I persist with this poem,
Mariana is quite likely to vanish from the poem altogether. The saints in
the stained glass, and the idea of martyrs suffering pain impassively,
have taken over as the dominant images. The process of writing is very

much about finding a subject. Writing about Mariana is the exercise, not necessarily an outcome in itself.

This activity should take you about 20 minutes.

Activity

Figure 4.4 is an iconic image from an edition of *Vogue* magazine from 1930, photographed by George Hoyningen-Huene (1900–68). Try using this image as the basis for some notes towards creating a poem, beginning by creating a series of statements in which there is a vowel-echo. You might like to try drafting the opening of a poem based on this photograph.

Figure 4.4   George Hoyningen-Huene, *Divers*. From *Vogue*, 5 July 1930. Photo: © Condé Nast Archives/Corbis.

Discussion

One of the decisions you will have had to make is who your speaker will be. One of the divers? The photographer? Yourself? Your representative? And what aspects of the photograph will you have focused upon? The stillness? The way their heads are turned away? The line of the horizon? The monochrome?

The poet Maura Dooley (b. 1957) used this photograph as the basis for her poem 'Bathers, 1930'.

Bathers, 1930

(from a photograph by George Hoyningen-Huene)

Staring so intently out to sea
they do not hear the stealthy camera
click like a key in a lock.

His hair is thick, sticky with salt.
Her hair is shingled. Their skins take a dip
in June sunlight. The air, the mood is blue.

The rest is out of focus; an ocean corrugates
and concertinas, the wind is a held breath,
the horizon too distant to believe in.

Their faces turned from us, they balance
on the edge of a narrow jetty. We look at them,
in black and white, from a long way off.

(Dooley, 1990, p. 61)

What Dooley has done in this poem is focus on the difficulty of interpreting the image, and (not unlike Draycott in 'Golf') on the way the couple is perpetually 'distant' or 'a long way off'. Notice also how the voice of this poem, which is reflective and reserved, is created for us by a quiet pattern of echoes, by the way the vowels recur and resonate, and even by the stealthy use of internal rhyme ('click'/'thick'/ 'sticky'). Dooley also shows us a very good example of where and why to break a line:

                                              they balance
    on the edge of a narrow jetty.

The line-break gives us a fractional moment in which to experience that sense of teetering on an edge. Another quality to take away from this poem is its careful use of contemporary word order and vocabulary.

4.7   The tone of poetic voice

Because I specified the use of long vowel sounds at the start of the 'Mariana' activity, I have, at least at this stage, dictated the tone of the drafts of the accompanying poem, which is one of weariness, of desultory introspection. The long vowel sounds have slowed the pace. The pattern of sound, and the accompanying rhythm could dictate an entirely different mood. To give you an example, if the voice was to be hesitant, I would expect there to be far more breaks, and more changes in pace.

> I might perhaps
>   suspect that
> a hesitant poem would
> use breaks
>
> more frequently, that it would
> vary the rhythms, or possess
>   a slightly unsettling
> and tentative pattern.

This activity should take you about 20 minutes.

Activity

See if you can create examples of short poetic extracts which aim to have one of the following kinds of voice:

angry	carefree	thoughtful	jaunty	mournful
precise	excitable	meditative	intimate	scatterbrained

The adjectives suggested are not mutually exclusive – feel free to combine two, if you wish, or to try others. Think about what kinds of rhythm you might use. Think also about the importance of echo.

Discussion

In the process of experiment, you probably considered most if not all of the following ways in which you might achieve the chosen voice, in addition to your use of echo and rhythm:

- whether the voice was your own, or the voice of someone else
- what kind of vocabulary you should use
- how many breaks or pauses you should introduce

- how you could imply the mood, rather than explain it
- whether to use end-rhyme, internal rhyme, half-rhyme
- the potential length of the piece
- how you might lay the piece out on the page.

4.8   A variety of voices

In this section I will give some examples of how contemporary writers have created voices that are (although I could use other adjectives) thoughtful, jaunty and angry – that have distinctive identities. After each type of voice is discussed, there is a brief activity (on which you should spend no longer than 15 minutes) that gives you the opportunity to try drafting a few lines in that voice. You will find the discussion for all three activities in this section at the end of the last activity.

Thoughtful

Achieving a thoughtful, perhaps quizzical tone of voice in a poem may mean writing in a looser, more clearly conversational tone, one in which there is a degree of intimacy set up with the reader. You can see this in the opening to the poem 'Forgetfulness' by Billy Collins (b. 1941), the whole of which you can hear him reading on DVD 2.

> The name of the author is the first to go
> followed obediently by the title, the plot,
> the heartbreaking conclusion, the entire novel
> which suddenly becomes one you have never read, never even
>   heard of,
>
> as if, one by one, the memories you used to harbor
> decided to retire to the southern hemisphere of the brain,
> to a little fishing village where there are no phones.
>
> Long ago you kissed the names of the nine Muses good-bye
> and watched the quadratic equation pack its bag,
> and even now as you memorize the order of the planets,
>
> something else is slipping away, a state flower perhaps,
> the address of an uncle, the capital of Paraguay.
>
> (Collins, 2001, p. 29)

The method here is to use a loose-limbed conversational rhythm – the fourth line here includes eight beats and eighteen syllables. This gives the voice a genial, almost casual tone, with the repetitions buried less ostentatiously in the lines: 'suddenly becomes', 'little fishing village', 'pack its bag', 'capital of Paraguay'. If you were to substitute another country (say, Turkey, Russia, Italy) for 'Paraguay', you would lose both the echo of 'capital' at the start of the country, and the open vowel, almost drawled, at the end of the line. Collins himself, discussing the teaching of poetry, has remarked that understanding tone is the key to meaning:

> I think teaching [students] how to read a poem involves conveying what tone is. And when you convey the tone, you're really conveying the spirit of the poem. That's more important than whatever passes for meaning. If they get the tone of voice, that's almost enough to direct them through the poem and replace or at least quiet the anxiety about what the poem means.
>
> (Collins, n.d.)

A similarly conversational tone is used by Michael Laskey (b. 1944) in his poem 'Lesson'.

Lesson

Five minutes, no more, our stroll
from the restaurant through the quiet
Sunday afternoon streets,
headed for our books, the next chapter
a bench in the park or stretched out
under trees on the grass. We were crossing
the Paseo del Prado when you noticed
my backpack gaping, unzipped,
the wallet gone, no longer mine.
Apparently it's always happening
with backpacks, but after the shock
and the hassle, it's the deftness
I'm left with, how I didn't feel a thing,
how you need to keep practising.

(Laskey, 2008, p. 100)

The thoughtful voice here is achieved by a great deal of understatement, and also by the intimacy of the address from 'I' to 'you', as if it were a private conversation (it is a more intimate poem altogether than Collins's poem). The movement across the lines is unobtrusive, and the rhythm mirrors the steady pace of the events. The words which denote pace – 'stroll', 'headed', 'crossing' – are not sudden at all, and the key word 'noticed' is undemonstrative. One of the key words defining the voice is 'Apparently'. There is a brief – very brief – moment recording the 'shock/and the hassle', in which the word 'shock', with its harder final consonant, appears at the end of the line. But the poem moves quietly forward, using the subtle echo of 'left' and 'deft' to turn the 'lesson' of the event into one quite opposite to what we might have imagined of the speaker. The lesson is not about learning to remember to zip your backpack, but an understanding of the practice that a thief must have to undertake – the lesson the thief must learn. The quiet near-rhymes of 'thing'/'practising' at the ends of the final two lines ensure that the voice remains quiet, meditative, discursive. If the last two lines had finished with the beat falling on a full rhyme (say, 'thing'/'sting'), the ending would have been too emphatic for the voice in the poem's purpose.

Activity

Write four or five lines of a draft poem in which, as in 'Lesson', you are describing something surprising, but doing so in a calm and thoughtful way. You are free to choose any subject, but here is one to try: a car passing you at great speed, forcing you to jump out of the way.

Jaunty

Jauntiness implies an up-tempo beat, and tempo is crucial to the identity of a poetic voice. The beat is plainly going to be more pronounced in an up-tempo poem. A jaunty voice is an enthusiastic voice, one that takes ostentatious pleasure in what it says. The two examples here, about examiners, allow you to see different vocal tactics at work. The first is an extract from 'Skipping Rhyme for Graduates', a poem by Sophie Hannah (b. 1971).

> I've got the motive.
> I've got the stamina.
> I'm going to kill
> The external examiner.
>
> Let crows and vultures
> Pick at the carcass
> After I've murdered
> The stingiest of markers.

Bring out the bin-bags.
Bring out the spades.
Bring down the evil sod
Who brings down the grades.

Give me an alibi.
Give me a gun.
Wanted a first
But I got a two-one.

(Hannah, 1995, p. 49)

As the title implies, this poem skips along with malicious glee. The repetitions now extend to rhyming, and the phrasal repetitions are much more ostentatious. The slangy vocabulary breezes the reader along. Notice here that Hannah uses the rhymes to give the emphasis: there is no internal echo on the vowel sounds, and only a little alliteration ('pick'/ 'carcass', 'bin-bags') to energise the sound of the poem. (Alliteration is in my view a very over-rated means of giving a poem a sense of wholeness.) The rhyme scheme is loose, too – ABCB – which helps us understand that this is a comic voice. By contrast, here is an extract from 'The Examiners' by John Whitworth (b. 1945) (the first and last stanzas of five).

Where the house is cold and empty and the garden's overgrown,
They are there.
Where the letters lie unopened by a disconnected phone,
They are there.
Where your footsteps echo strangely on each moonlit
    cobblestone,
Where a shadow streams behind you but the shadow's not your
    own,
You may think the world's your oyster but it's bone, bone, bone:
They are there, they are there, they are there.

[…]
They are there, they are there like a whisper on the air,
They are there.
They are slippery and soapy with our hope and our despair,
They are there.
So it's idle if we bridle or pretend we never care,
If the questions are superfluous and the marking isn't fair,
For we know they're going to get us, we just don't know when
    or where,
They are there, they are there, they are there.

(Whitworth, 2007, p. 21)

This is a sinister voice, but at the same time it is comically sinister, because of the sheer extent of the rhyme and echo. The first stanza offers us two rhymes – and uses four *-one* end-rhymes, which it reinforces with the repetition of 'bone', and four, arguably five, further long *o* sounds (because it is very tempting here to give a long *o* to disconnected). What you will have to decide is whether you think the voice is sufficiently sinister to create a momentary frisson or fright. In the last stanza, it uses the refrain *-ere* (pronounced 'air') rhyme no fewer than thirteen times. I would argue that it is the voice of a music-hall or stage villain, partly because of the ostentation of internal rhymes like 'idle' and 'bridle', and partly because of the contrasting rhythms – the tiptoeing, pattering rhythm of the long lines and the short, slightly melodramatic refrains. But the voice is certainly more disturbing than the voice in Hannah's poem.

Activity

Write two lines to match the line below, making sure that the beat is lively and that the same rhyme is used at the end of each line. Start each line, as I do with the first one, with the phrase 'Open up'. You can write on any subject, but if you'd rather, use anything that is suggested by the title 'Under Arrest'.

> Open up the window with a hammer or a chisel ...

Angry

Outright, splenetic rage is exceptionally hard to manage in a poem. Controlled anger, which will carry more force, and run less risk of being comic, needs to be emphatic, direct. The poem 'A Cold Coming' by Tony Harrison (b. 1937), inspired by the image of the charred head of an Iraqi soldier in a blown-up vehicle, was published in a national newspaper during the First Gulf War in 1991 (it was reprinted in 2003). It opens with the following lines:

> I saw the charred Iraqi lean towards me from bomb-blasted screen,
> his windscreen wiper like a pen ready to write down thoughts for men,

his windscreen wiper like a quill he's reaching for to make his
    will.

I saw the charred Iraqi lean like someone made of Plasticine

as though he'd stopped to ask the way and this is what I heard
    him say:

'Don't be afraid I've picked on you for this exclusive interview.

Isn't it your sort of poet's task to find words for this frightening
    mask?

If that gadget that you've got records words from such scorched
    vocal cords,

press RECORD before some dog devours me mid-monologue.'

(Harrison, 2003 [1991], p. 12)

In this poem, which, to return to the theme of Book 1, possesses
considerable authority, the bitterness is controlled by the rhymes (which
appear halfway through the lines), and by the general firmness of the
rhythm. Harrison makes the most of his invective by repeating phrases
and also sounds (in 'charred Iraqi', and 'windscreen wiper', for
instance), and by not only using a colloquial, naturally ordered language,
but also by including direct and monosyllabic phrases ('and this is what
I heard him say'). It is intense and fierce; but it does not shout. As with
Michael Longley's poem 'Ceasefire', which you read in Chapter 3 of
Book 1, the authority of this poem was extended by its publication in a
national newspaper, and also by the publication next to it of the grim
photograph that inspired it.

Harrison's savage poem is both personal and political. There are other
kinds of anger, as in this extract from 'Ill-Wishing Him' by Dorothy
Nimmo (1932–2001), in which a wife sardonically recounts what she
wishes had happened to a husband who has left her.

I wish he'd had to rent a room
in Peterborough, to take his washing
to the launderette, watch his shirts turn pink.
I wish he'd lived on pork-pie and pizza
and it had made him sick.

> I wish he'd gone senile and forgotten
> who he was and what he'd done
> and every day I could remind him. I wish
> he'd died and left my name
> as next of kin. They'd ring me
> and I'd say, *Never heard of him.*

(Nimmo, 2000, p. 12)

Once again, notice the importance of the repetitions at both the phrasal ('I wish') and syllable level ('w*a*sh'/'w*a*tch', '*i*t'/'s*i*ck', 'k*i*n'/'r*i*ng'), and the accessibility of the language. The poetic voice is made stronger by the incremental nature of the curses. It makes the voice vicious and comic at the same time.

Activity

Find a story or an article in a daily newspaper in which one person is complaining about the actions of another (this should not be hard!). Write the draft opening of a poem – four or five lines – in which you use the voice of the complainant to express your anger with the other person. Think of a repetitive phrase that will bind the opening together.

Discussion

In each of the three activities in this section, you have been experimenting with creating a first draft. In each case, you have been asked to make a conscious effort to use rhythm, repetition or beat to establish the tone. In other words, you have been asked to make a conscious effort to create a voice, much more conscious than if you were simply talking to someone or writing a casual email or letter, and more conscious too than if you were writing prose. Poetry is a more conscious art-form, as I suggested above: the trick is not to make it self-conscious. That is not to say that the use of words is never ostentatious. Poetic voices are by nature ostentatious – the degree of ostentation depends on the nature of the voice you are creating.

4.9   Creating voices of authority

In Book 1, you looked at notions of authority. What may have struck you is how often the texts cited as possessing authority are in poetic form – perhaps implying that poetry is often considered to be the medium through which different kinds of authority are expressed.

The kind of authority I have in mind is not the poetry which is, as it were, licensed by the state. The long history of the laureateship in Great Britain has never been known to produce poems of any special character (see the box on laureateship for a brief note on this). For instance, in 1852 Tennyson wrote an ode on the Duke of Wellington, published on the morning of his funeral, that begins

> Bury the Great Duke
>   With an empire's lamentation;
> Let us bury the Great Duke
>   To the noise of the mourning of a mighty nation;
> Mourning when their leaders fall,
> Warriors carry the warrior's pall,
> And sorrow darkens hamlet and hall.

(Tennyson, 1963 [1852], p. 156)

The ode continues for a further 274 lines. It was received with 'all but Universal deprecation' (Hibbert, 1998, p. 402). Almost all laureate poems have received a less than enthusiastic response, although the incumbent, Carol Ann Duffy, has been praised for her work.

Laureateship

The post of poet laureate is a royal appointment, with a history going back at least to the seventeenth century and probably much further, to the thirteenth century, or even earlier. The duties of the laureate were, historically, to write public poetry in honour or celebration of national events.

From 1670 to 1998, the post was for life. In 1998, tenure was limited to ten years, and the second to hold the post under this rule is Carol Ann Duffy, the first woman to be given the post. She has promised to be more wide-ranging in her choice of subject.

There have been many poets who have turned the post down, including Thomas Gray (1716–71), who said he would rather be 'pin-maker to the palace'. William Wordsworth (1770–1850) took the post on the strict condition that he would not be obliged to write any laureate verse. (He never did.)

In poetry, the authority of a voice will often come not from its public but its private quality. It will come from its intimacy, and, if it is to carry any real power, from a mixture of complexity and emotional honesty. An authoritative voice is one that requires you to listen, not merely to hear.

The authority of a writer stems, too, not from the depiction of character but from the clarity and emotional force of the writer's voice, a voice that should be neither strident nor didactic nor dogmatic. What the reader responds to is the control and force of the language, the manipulation of voice so that it conducts and encourages debate. In contemporary poetry, this might well be called a degree of truth, a presentation of language that is at once intimate and colloquial while also formally compelling. To put it more simply, the poetry has to be distinctive and personal.

This activity should take you about 20 minutes.

Activity

Read the poem 'Honour Killing' by Imtiaz Dharker (b. 1954) in Reading 4.4. Can you suggest ways in which the voice she uses might be said to carry authority? Think about the way the lines and stanzas are arranged, the way that the poem develops, the language that it uses. When you have read the poem, watch Dharker reading it on DVD 2. How does her reading affect your view of the text?

Discussion

In my view, what gives this poem authority is that it fuses the public and the personal. We hear the speaker, but we also understand what the writer's attitude is to her, a mixture of empathy and pain for her predicament. Indeed, perhaps we can't be sure who is 'taking off' the coat, veil, silks – it might be Dharker herself, it might be the speaker she has created. Many tactics are used here. The tone is cool and collected, at odds with the subject, which seems to be about a woman discarding her nationality, her faith, her marriage and then, more surreally, her physical self. The tension between the tone and the subject is what forces the reader to concentrate: this too gives the poem authority.

The vocabulary is not complex. Perhaps some of us would need to be told what a mangalsutra is (a golden ornament tied by thread around the neck of a bride, by the bridegroom, in a Hindu wedding ceremony), but the poem is highly accessible. This too gives it authority. So too does the repetition, the incantation of the poem, the repeated lines 'I'm taking off …', which lead to the repeated 'Let's see …'. The repetition is also present at a more subliminal level – the repetition of 'black', the repetition of 'that' and 'what', the repetition of the sounds in 'sw*ore*'/'w*ore*', 'f*eed*'/ 'n*eed*s', 'squ*eeze*'/'*eas*y', the concluding short *o* sound in '*plot*ting' and '*geog*raphy'. These repetitions feed the intensity of the poem, which arrives, through the ambiguity of 'plotting', at a moment of decision. The poem possesses what I referred to above: emotional honesty. And, troublingly perhaps, we are kept in check throughout the poem by that title: 'Honour Killing'. We have to decide what is happening. We might wonder what sparked the poem (which was the murder, by her own family, of a woman who wanted a divorce). However, notice that Dharker, who is a Scots Muslim by birth, but whose partner is Hindu, does not direct us in a journalistic way. The voice does not belong to a specific woman, but to a representative of all women. No mention of specific faith is made. The poem has authority because it does not offer an argument but an exploration, and because it develops in a quizzical and unpredictable way, the stanzas shortening as it comes to its point.

I would also argue that the poem is given added authority by Dharker's performance of it: that the power of a poem is enhanced by the quiet drama of being spoken aloud (all the more authoritative for not being 'read', either from a text or a prompter). It is worth noting that the filming, by Pamela Robertson-Pearce, observes the reading in an intimate, informal setting. It does not attempt to dramatise the poem with images. It lets the poet and the poem do their work.

4.10   Writing with authority

Dharker's poem offers you many examples of how to invest writing with authority: repetition; echo; tension; simplicity of language, but a degree of complexity; development; a personal subject with broader political implications. Perhaps it also carries authority because it possesses only partially suppressed rage. And, of course, its authority comes from the fact that it is attacking another authority. In the next activity you can use some of these techniques to produce some writing of your own.

This activity should take you about 30 minutes.

Activity

Choose a subject about which you feel passionate. It might come from something you have read about, or even something that has happened to you – but beware the side-effect of writing something very personal. Writing directly about your own life may prevent you from distancing yourself from the subject sufficiently. When you have chosen your subject, set down what you feel about it in the form of a series of statements, beginning, if you like, 'This is …' or 'Whenever I …'. Don't worry about making your statements rhyme. What you should have at the end of the activity is the framework for a poem, not necessarily a poem itself.

Discussion

What you have written is the draft of what is known as a 'list poem', and sometimes as a 'litany poem', in which successive statements repeat, amend, expand and amplify earlier ones. If you look back at the versions of the *Metta Sutta* in Chapter 1 of Book 1, especially the Amaravati version (in Section 1.5), you'll see that this kind of repetition is a characteristic of many religious chants or songs.

The poem 'Spider' by Geoff Hattersley (b. 1956), an elegy to a spider he has just squashed, is a parody of the same technique – making fun by exploring the spider's non-human existence, while at the same time investigating the very human attributes it lacks, all the while repeating 'It never…' at the opening of each line.

> The spider was completely unprepared
> for assault from above by an ash-tray,
> it never had a friend it could count on.

It never knew its blood-group.
It never saw itself changing, or any need to.
It never said: 'No more excuses.'
It never felt tempted by drugs.
It never knew the itch to the nearest bar.
Its earning power was never an issue.
It was never hurt by a few home-truths.
It never did anything for anyone.
It never knew the myth of Wyatt Earp.
It never hoped for more than was likely.
It never had Watchtower thrust at it.
It never saw a rainbow, or a bunch of flowers
dropped into an open grave.
It never wrote an essay on the works of Alexander Pope.
It never filled in an application form.
It never married for love or money.
It never had a honeymoon in a hotel.
It never knew who was Prime Minister.
It never knew if it was lucky or not.
It never shopped for clothes.
It never smiled.
It never felt like a paperclip
in a jar in a cupboard in a shed.
It never carried a briefcase.
It never missed the last train.
It never slept off a hangover.
It never thought it was Marlon Brando.

(Hattersley, 1994, p. 47)

What gives authority to Hattersley's enjoyably daft poem (which
continues for a further ninety lines) is the resonance of repetition. If
you work on your own piece, seeing if you can put the statements in the
most interesting order, you will have a poem on your hands, and one
that has the authority not just of the written word but of incantation –
by implication, the spoken voice.

4.11   Developing a subject for a poem

In this chapter so far, you have looked at the way that poetry, as a verbal art, is highly conscious of its use of language, and is more conscious of itself as possessing an invented voice, one that is shaped, rhythmic, musical. But understanding the technique might reasonably be said to be secondary to having a subject about which to write a poetic text. As I have suggested with the 'Mariana' activity, a poem can start in one place, and take the writer into a different, surprising direction. There are many techniques for activating the creative impulse, and space precludes listing them all here.

However, there are two particular ways of doing this. One is to begin with a constraint – it might be a specific form, it might be using a picture as a starting point. You might have been surprised to learn from the interview with Jane Draycott on DVD 2 that her poem 'Golf', which you looked at earlier in the chapter, is one of a sequence of twenty-six poems based on the words used by the NATO Phonetic Alphabet, which uses code-words for letters: alpha, bravo, charlie, delta, echo, foxtrot, golf, etc. What Draycott has done is to force her imagination to work by challenging it: the title is dictated by the sequence of the code-words. She has forced herself to draw observations and images out of the game of golf, in which she has no inherent interest. The constraint of the title is what forces her to think, to create.

While it is true that there are many famous long narrative poems in the English language, most poems are comparatively short. This is because they find their voice by focusing on an incident (the dropping of an ashtray on a spider, the theft of a wallet from a backpack, seeing a photo of two bathers). Poems, as texts, are very much about capturing and interpreting a moment, and seeing what potential for exploration there is within that moment. It may help to think of a poem as a photograph, rather than as a film narrative. In poetry, creative writing is often sparked by a single image, one that is given added resonance by the kinds of tricks of sound and rhythm explored above.

4.12 Experimenting with language

The poetic voices to which you have been introduced so far have been reasonably and recognisably conversational, but, as the prose extracts in Reading 4.1 show, voices can be more complex, more subtle, more experimental with language. As long as you think the reader will understand what you write, there is no reason why the language should not become more elliptical, more concentrated. This final example suggests the extent to which poetry can bring together meaning and melody until part of its quality is purely sonic.

Activity

1 Look at Figure 4.5. What tactics might you use to give voice to the fish in this photograph?

2 Turn to Reading 4.5 and read the poem 'Shoal' by the Australian poet Les Murray (b. 1938), which is spoken not by a single voice but by a shoal of fish. How has Murray created the voice? What techniques can you see him using?

This activity should take you about 20 minutes.

Discussion

This is a more tricky voice to explore, and not only because the shoal thinks and speaks in 'unison'. However, you can see that the poem operates on one level as a liquid soundscape, almost as pure sound, with its rhythms mimicking the changes of direction taken by a shoal of fish, and the repeated and punning 'I'/'eye' references. If you read the poem aloud, you will feel the way the poem wheels – and you will also notice that the poem rhymes, using only five end-rhyme sounds in its nineteen lines, and deliberately varying where they fall, to capture the unpredictable shifting of a shoal. You will also see that Murray has used practically the full range of internal rhyme, half-rhyme, near-rhyme and echo to capture the way the shoal swirls. Murray also compresses the language, editing out some words to create a sense of mass.

Yet of course there is a hidden voice behind the voice of the fish in this poem: the voice of the speaker or poet – telling us, for instance, that the fish respond collectively to 'tasting …/vague umbrations of chemical'. 'Umbrations' is a very rare word for 'faint indications': the fish, so Murray tells us, react constantly and instinctively to pollutants, and also, never stop this process of reacting: hence 'the pure' or steady movement is always 'inimical', or potentially hostile. In a technique reminiscent of the

Figure 4.5   Shoal of fish, Tubbataha, Philippines. Photographed by Martin Strmiska. Photo: © Martin Strmiska/Alamy.

passage from Thomas's *Under Milk Wood* in Reading 4.1, Murray invents the compound word 'earblades'. He uses this to describe the way the fish use their own inner sonar to watch out for predators, like the redfin (a type of perch, which is known to have caused huge damage to fish stocks since being introduced to Australia). The dash at the end of the poem perhaps indicates that the redfin has struck again.

In this dense and dazzling poem, Murray has insinuated his own voice into the voice of the shoal. We can see the voice as the voice of the shoal, and yet we can also hear Murray's voice, exploring the choral nature of the creatures and their movement.

Murray's poem has inspired a musical piece by the Australian composer Damien Ricketson, a piece which is for six unaccompanied voices. You can hear the piece on DVD 2. What Ricketson has done is to move from voices with a text to voices that verge on pure sound. What this illustrates about the poetic voice is that it is at heart made up of the sounds of words, and that what makes a poetic voice doubly distinctive is the added attention the creative writer pays to the patterns of words, not least at the redrafting stage.

Conclusion

In this chapter, we have looked at the way in which writing 'poetic language', and writing poetry itself, means harnessing a variety of techniques. We have also explored how these poetic techniques mean introducing subtle new resonance into writing, resonance that uses language in a consciously inventive way, one that moves closer along a continuum towards music. Finally, we have looked at creative writing in a way that is intended to show that writing and reading are inseparable: testing yourself as a creative writer means that you will be a more informed reader, just as being a more informed reader will make you a more successful creative writer.

References

Aristotle (1996) *Poetics* (trans. M. Heath), London, Penguin.

Beckett, S. (1999 [1976]) *For to End Yet Again*, London, John Calder.

Collins, B. (n.d.) Interview [online], http://www.critiquemagazine.com/onwriting/collins_b.html (accessed 12 November 2009).

Collins, B. (2001) *Sailing Alone Around the Room*, New York, Random House.

Dharker, I. (2008) 'Honour Killing' in Astley, N. (ed.) *In Person: 30 Poets*, Tarset, Bloodaxe.

Dooley, M. (1990) *Explaining Magnetism*, Newcastle upon Tyne, Bloodaxe.

Draycott, J. (2009) *Over*, Manchester, Carcanet.

Duffy, C.A. (1991) *The Other Country*, Manchester, Anvil.

Gunn, T. (2005–2010) 'Considering the Snail', *The Poetry Archive* [online], http://www.poetryarchive.org/poetryarchive/singlePoem.do?poemId=7414 (accessed 25 August 2010).

Gunn, T. (2007) *Selected Poems*, London, Faber and Faber.

Hannah, S. (1995) *The Hero and the Girl Next Door*, Manchester, Carcanet.

Harrison, T. (2003 [1991]) 'A Cold Coming', *The Guardian*, 14 February, p. 12; also available online at http://www.guardian.co.uk/theguardian/2003/feb/14/features11.g2 (accessed 25 August 2010).

Hattersley, G. (1994) *Don't Worry*, Newcastle upon Tyne, Bloodaxe.

Hibbert, C. (1998) *Wellington: A Personal History*, London, HarperCollins.

Laskey, M. (2008) *The Man Alone*, Sheffield, Smith/Doorstop.

Lavery, B. (1987) *Origin of the Species* in Remnant, M. (ed.) *Plays by Women*, vol. 6, London, Methuen.

Lavery, B. (2007 [2000]) *A Wedding Story* in *Plays 1*, London, Faber and Faber.

Mitchell, J. (1997) *The Complete Poems and Lyrics*, London, Chatto & Windus.

Murray, L. (1993) *Translations from the Natural World*, Manchester, Carcanet.

Nimmo, D. (2000) *The Wigbox*, Huddersfield, Smith/Doorstop.

Szirtes, G. (2004) *Reel*, Tarset, Bloodaxe.

Tennyson, A. (1963 [1852]) *Selected Poems*, Oxford, Oxford University Press.

Thomas, D. (1992 [1954]) *Under Milk Wood*, London, Orion.

Whitworth, J. (2007) 'The Examiners', *The Times Literary Supplement*, 13 July, issue 5441, p. 21.

Further reading

Whitworth, J. (2006) *Writing Poetry*, London, A & C Black.

Sansom, P. (1994) *Writing Poems*, Newcastle upon Tyne, Bloodaxe.

Oliver, M. (1994) *A Poetry Handbook*, Orlando, Harcourt.

Astley, N. (ed.) (2008) *In Person: 30 Poets*, Tarset, Bloodaxe.

Readings

Reading 4.1: Three examples of experimental prose

Example 1

Ruinstrewn land, he has trodden it all night long, I gave up, hugging the hedges, between road and ditch, on the scant grass, little slow steps, no sound, stopping ever and again, every ten steps say, little wary steps, to catch his breath, then listen, ruinstrewn land, I gave up before birth, it is not possible otherwise, but birth there had to be, it was he, I was inside, now he stops again, for the hundredth time that night say, that gives the distance gone, it's the last, hunched over his stick, ...

Source: Beckett, S. (1999 [1976]) *For to End Yet Again*, London, John Calder, p. 39.

Example 2

The boys are dreaming wicked or of the bucking ranches of the night and the jollyrodgered sea. And the anthracite statues of the horses sleep in the fields, and the cows in the byres, and the dogs in the wet-nosed yard; and the cats nap in the slant corners or lope sly, streaking and needling, on the one cloud of the roofs.

Source: Thomas, D. (1992 [1954]) *Under Milk Wood*, London, Orion, pp. 1–2.

Example 3

he was called
Plato Aristotle Copernicus Galileo
Bacon Descartes Newton
and because he was so interested in clocks he began to take apart other clocks man clocks woman clocks animal clocks plant clocks so soon his home was littered and strewn
with pieces
of the different clocks
and the odd thing was
the more he took the clocks apart
with his sharp instruments

the less they seemed to work
the less they ticked
the stiller the cogs and wheels
were ...

Source: Lavery, B. (1987) *Origin of the Species* in Remnant, M. (ed.) *Plays by Women*, vol. 6, London, Methuen, p. 81.

Reading 4.2: from 'Amelia'

I was driving across the burning desert
When I spotted six jet planes
Leaving six white vapor trails across the bleak terrain
It was the hexagram of the heavens
It was the strings of my guitar
Amelia, it was just a false alarm

The drone of flying engines
Is a song so wild and blue
It scrambles time and seasons if it gets through to you
Then your life becomes a travelogue
Of picture-post-card-charms
Amelia, it was just a false alarm.

Source: Mitchell, J. (1997) *The Complete Poems and Lyrics*, London, Chatto & Windus, p. 158.

Reading 4.3: 'Golf'

In the mirage we saw three figures, kings
perhaps or the type with the migrant gene –
adventurous, always one step ahead

striking a path through the desert simply
by instinct, first to smell the oasis,
first then to gaze on the moon in the well.

We struck out towards them. It felt as if
boundless and bare the morning might take us
and carry us elsewhere, somewhere ahead

which wasn't a carpet of dandelions
struck by the clock of the wind again and again
and no one to blame but yourself.

Between us and the men who looked like us
a river, an ocean of sand, a gulf.

Source: Draycott, J. (2009) *Over*, Manchester, Carcanet, p. 47.

Reading 4.4: 'Honour Killing'

At last I'm taking off this coat,
  this black coat of a country
  that I swore for years was mine,
  that I wore more out of habit
  than design.
  Born wearing it,
  I believed I had no choice.

I'm taking off this veil,
  this black veil of a faith
  that made me faithless
  to myself,
  that tied my mouth,
  gave my god a devil's face,
  and muffled my own voice.

I'm taking off these silks,
  these lacy things
  that feed dictator dreams,
  the mangalsutra and the rings
  rattling in a tin cup of needs
  that beggared me.

I'm taking off this skin,
  and then the face, the flesh,
  the womb.

Let's see
  what I am in here
  when I squeeze past
  the easy cage of bone.

Let's see
  what I am out here,
  making, crafting,
  plotting
  at my new geography.

Source: Dharker, I. (2008) 'Honour Killing' in Astley, N. (ed.) *In Person: 30 Poets*, Tarset, Bloodaxe, p. 59.

Reading 4.5: 'Shoal'

Eye-and-eye eye an eye
each. What blinks is I,
unison of the whole shoal. Thinks:
a dark idea circling by –
again the eyes' I winks.
Eye-and-eye near no eye
is no I, though gill-pulse drinks
and nervy fins spacewalk. Jinx
jets the jettisoned back into all,
tasting, each being a tongue,
vague umbrations of chemical:
this way thrilling, that way Wrong,
the pure always inimical,
compound being even the sheer thing
I suspend I in, and thrust
against, for speed and feeding,
all earblades for the eel's wave-gust
over crayfishes' unpressured beading,
for bird-dive boom, redfin's gaped gong –

Source: Murray, L. (1993) *Translations from the Natural World*, Manchester, Carcanet, p. 22.

Afterword

Philip Seargeant

Afterword

At one point in Jonathan Swift's novel *Gulliver's Travels* the hero finds himself in a city called Lagado, where he is given a tour of a scientific academy. There he is shown a number of innovative projects for the betterment of mankind. These include such bizarre things as a device for extracting sunbeams from cucumbers and a radical new method of architecture intended to revolutionise the building of houses 'by beginning at the Roof and working downwards to the Foundation' (2003 [1726], p. 168). At the academy's School of Language, he is introduced to a scheme for 'entirely abolishing Words altogether' (p. 172). Instead of speaking, people will simply carry around all the objects they are likely to want to refer to, and then produce them one by one when they wish to 'say' anything. The only apparent drawback with this is that if a person wants to have an extended conversation, the collection of objects he or she needs to carry around is likely to become a little cumbersome. As Gulliver comments:

> I have often beheld two of those Sages almost sinking under the Weight of their Packs, like Peddlers amongst us; who when they met in the Streets would lay down their Loads, open their Sacks and hold Conversation for an Hour together; then put up their Implements, help each other to resume their Burthens, and take their Leave.
>
> (Swift, 2003 [1726], pp. 172–4)

The underlying principle on which this scheme is based is that 'Words are only Names for *Things*' (p. 172). Swift's book is a satire, and in this episode he is parodying the world of science and academia. But although his general approach to this system of communication is one of mockery, the underlying conception of how language works (that 'words are names for things') is still, in fact, a popular and widespread one. The idea that languages consist of vast hoards of words, all of which stand for something out there in the world, and that their main purpose is to relay factual information, is not at all uncommon. In fact, one of the people Swift is satirising here is the great seventeenth-century philosopher John Locke, who was a strong proponent of this view.

As we have seen over the course of this book, however, human language is far more multifaceted than this. The eighteenth-century German thinker Wilhelm von Humboldt wrote that human language is a system which 'makes infinite use of finite means' (quoted in Chomsky, 1965, p. v). That is, from a palette of basic sounds (the vowels and consonants that we looked at in Chapter 4), or from the relatively small group of letters that make up the alphabet, we are able to put together complex utterances that can articulate an almost infinite number of things. Furthermore, language doesn't *only* represent objects out there in the world. It expresses feelings, ideas, emotions and aspects of identity, and is also used as a form of action which helps us get things done. How, for example, from a bundle of objects carried around on one's back would one be able to say 'I'm sorry about that', or 'Would you mind if we take a rain check and perhaps reschedule for next Thursday', let alone express the range of feelings that can be achieved in a sonnet or a song?

Over the course of this book we have looked at many of these multifaceted elements of language, and at how they are used in acts of expression. A key theme has been the way that meaning is conveyed not simply by the content of utterances (i.e. by the way the words refer to things and ideas in the world), but also by their form and structure. The sounds of words, the manner in which they are combined, the expectations they produce in an audience, all contribute to the overall meaning of the utterance. We have seen how this happens in a variety of textual and communicative genres, ranging from newspaper reports and job interviews to popular songs and poetry. We have also looked at how language operates as a marker of identity and how the type of language a person speaks (in terms of accent, dialect and choice of register) has a strong relationship to the communities to which that person belongs. In the second part of the book we looked at strategies that creative writers employ to exploit the expressive potential of language and at how they play with language and edit and reshape it to create images and characters, voices and stories. In Chapter 4 we looked at instances of composition where the manipulation of language is able to achieve an almost musical effect, and where the referential content of the words (what they 'mean' in terms of objects and concepts) is secondary to the patterns of sound achieved by their artful arrangement. If language were reduced to a scheme that did nothing more than refer to objects out there in the real world, none of this would be possible. Language would be a mundane and limited tool, instead of the rich and adaptive resource it actually is.

Another key issue that has emerged is that this type of meaning can also have a powerful social and political effect. People are constantly being evaluated in terms of their use of language, whether from the type of accent they have or the way they answer a question in a job interview. Newspapers frame a view of the world through the way they organise the language of their reports. And creative writers can draw on forms of indirect meaning to express the complexities of human experience, as, for example, in Imtiaz Dharker's poem 'Honour Killing'. Often the subtleties of this type of meaning are not immediately apparent. They are hidden in the structure of a piece of discourse, in the subtext of a narrative, or in the interplay of form and content in a poem. By looking at how the process of expression happens, though, and at the nature of the resources that we use to communicate, we can gain a better idea of what is involved in the creation of texts, and of how they operate as powerful means of both personal and social expression.

We continue this analysis of the way that written language mediates the social world in Book 3, where the focus turns to the role played by different types of texts – political tracts, social histories and novels – in the debates and dialogues that created the political sensibilities of a particular historical period: mid-Victorian Britain. For this purpose we switch academic disciplines once again, to History and Literature, and examine how these can be used to illuminate the role played by voices and texts in the representation of a society's cultural and political history.

References

Chomsky, N. (1965) *Aspects of the Theory of Syntax*, Cambridge, MA, MIT Press.

Swift, J. (2003 [1726]) *Gulliver's Travels*, London, Penguin.

Glossary

academic register

see **register**.

accent

the features of pronunciation that indicate a person's regional or social background. The term refers specifically to pronunciation, while the term **dialect** is used to refer to differences in **grammar** and vocabulary.

audience

can conventionally mean those who watch a play (although it actually means 'listening'!) or film. However, it is often used as a general term for anyone for whom a creative writer composes. For example, we can talk of a novelist's audience.

back-story

the events that have taken place before the action of a story starts, and that we learn about during the story.

code-switching

the way in which speakers in bilingual situations can alternate from one language to another during the course of a conversation. Code-mixing is a similar process, but the switch between languages happens within a sentence rather than between sentences or **utterances**.

dialect

a language variety in which aspects of the vocabulary and **grammar** indicate a person's regional or social background. It is contrasted with **accent**, which refers specifically to differences in pronunciation.

dialogue

conversation between two or more characters.

discourse

a term that has a variety of slightly different meanings related to Language Studies. In this module, it's being used to refer to sequences of connected speech or writing, usually made up of more than one sentence.

discourse community

a social group who have common interests and who use a particular **register** of language (composed of specialist vocabulary and particular **genres**) when they are pursuing those interests.

drafting

the process of writing and rewriting through which a writer goes in the process of composing.

free indirect speech

a technique for allowing the reader to see into a character's mind, even when a piece of fiction is written in the third person.

genre

in the context of Language Studies, the term 'genre' refers to the different types of communicative act, which are distinguished from each other by the form they take and the purpose they have. For example, a letter is a particular type of genre, as is a job interview or a political speech. In each case, there are conventional patterns in the way the communicative act is organised, and the purpose it is designed to fulfil. In the context of Literature and Creative Writing, 'genre' has two related meanings. It can mean a particular type of writing, for instance, poetry, fiction, life writing, drama. It can also mean a subset of these, so that in fiction it could mean a novel or short story, or particular types of these, such as romance, crime, horror, fantasy, etc. (The term 'genre fiction' is often used to describe what are properly sub-genres.) Poetry might be lyric poetry or comic poetry or narrative poetry, and so on. Drama might be divided by medium, so that the word 'genre' could be used of screenplay, stage play, radio play.

genre fiction

see **genre**.

grammar

the way a language is structured. It is often used to refer in particular to the way in which words and their component parts (e.g. word endings that denote tense) combine to form sentences.

idiolect

the distinct pattern of language used by an individual speaker. It is often manifest in the use of particular items of vocabulary or idioms, as well as in pronunciation and **grammar**.

International Phonetic Alphabet (IPA)

a specialised system for transcribing the speech sounds of language.

language variation

the way in which the forms and structures of a language vary according to its users and to the circumstances in which it is used.

life writing

an umbrella term that covers autobiography and biography. It often uses techniques associated with fiction, and there are particular strands of it that are individually identified, such as travel writing. Its central focus is, as the term implies, the story of all or part of a life.

linguistics

the term used for the general study of language.

metaphor

a figure of speech in which two different things are implicitly compared, as in 'the grass bristled'; see also **simile**.

mode

the actual means by which a message is communicated. For example, the mode could be speech (the use of the voice), or writing, or, in the case of sign language, gestures. Different modes of communication have different possibilities and limitations, which result in different forms of language being associated with them.

narrator

the person who relays a story to readers. The narrator may be an uninvolved voice created by the writer, who 'knows' all or most of what takes place. It may be a character in the story, perhaps the central character 'speaking' in the first person. Choice of narrator is a strategy chosen by a creative writer to influence how the reader receives the story.

official language

a language that has a special legal status in a country, and is used in administration and education contexts.

oral history theatre

a general term for dramas that are created out of material spoken or written by real people. There are different kinds of oral history theatre, including verbatim theatre, which aims to edit together original words with minimum, or even no, alteration.

phonology

the study of the sound systems of languages.

plot

the ordering of events in a story.

prestige variety

a social dialect or accent that has a high status within society.

register

a variety of language that is defined according to its use in particular social contexts. It is often characterised by the use of specialist vocabulary or jargon. Register can be distinguished from **dialect** in that the former is a variety defined by its uses (i.e. what one is talking about), while the latter is a variety defined by its users (i.e. who is doing the talking). For example, an academic register is the type of language use that is appropriate in academic contexts (e.g. writing essays and assignments). It will consist of the use of specialised vocabulary, a certain level of formality of expression and a particular structuring of the text (e.g. the use of an essay format, which will include an introduction, a main body built around a central argument, a conclusion, and a list of references).

script

a fabricated piece of spoken language (i.e. one composed by a writer) which is designed to be performed by actors.

show

showing and telling are two different methods of developing a story. 'Showing' allows the reader to infer what is happening; 'telling' explains to the reader what is happening.

simile

a figure of speech in which two different things are explicitly compared, using the words 'like', 'as', or other direct connectives (e.g. 'the colour of'); see also **metaphor**.

sociolinguistics

the study of language use in society. It is contrasted with general **linguistics**, which views language as an abstract system and concentrates particularly on the structure of this system. Sociolinguistics, on the other hand, examines the relationship between language and social life.

standard language

the variety of language that is predominantly used in broadcasting and education. A standard language does not exhibit regional variation, and is often used as the official variety within a society. It is considered to be a **prestige variety**.

stanza

stanza and verse are often used to mean the same thing – a section of a poem. However, 'stanza' is more commonly used of poetry, and 'verse' of song.

subtext

what characters may be thinking, despite what they are saying.

tell

see **show**.

transcript

a written representation of a piece of spoken **discourse**.

utterance

a complete unit of speech used by someone when speaking, and often proceeded and followed by a space of silence, or by a change of speaker.

verbatim theatre

see **oral history theatre**.

vernacular

when language is 'in the vernacular', it means that the language draws on the everyday, colloquial patterns of speech, as against a more formal style of expression.

verse

see **stanza**.

Watergate

the Watergate Hotel, which gives its name to the scandal known as 'Watergate', is in Washington, DC. In 1972, a presidential election year, the Democratic Party headquarters, situated at the hotel, were found to have been wire-tapped and robbed. Over the next two years, investigations traced the intrusions to an organisation set up to re-elect Richard Nixon as president (he duly won the election). Nixon was forced to resign after it was discovered that there was a tape machine installed in the Oval Office which recorded all conversations, recordings which Nixon was reluctant to release. The recordings revealed that Nixon had attempted to cover up the crime, not that he had instigated it. The suffix '-gate' is still routinely added to almost any political or other scandal.

Acknowledgements

Grateful acknowledgement is made to the following sources.

Text

Reading 1.1: Tan, A. (1990) 'Mother tongue', *The Threepenny Review*, No. 43, Autumn 1990; © Amy Tan. Reading 1.2: *English with an accent*, Lippi-Green, R; Copyright 1997 Taylor & Francis Books Ltd. Reproduced by permission of Taylor and Francis Books UK. Reading 2.1: Swales, J.M. (1990) *Genre Analysis*; Cambridge University Press. Reading 2.2: Bakhtin, M. (1986) *Speech Genres and Other Late Essays*; University of Texas Press. Reading 2.3: Roberts, C. (2010) 'Institutional discourse', Maybin, J. and Swann, J. (eds) *The Routledge Companion to English Language Studies*; Routledge. Reading 2.4: © Brian Dooley. Reading 3.1: Robison, M. (1977) 'Pretty Ice'; Days; © Mary Robison. Reading 3.2: McInnes, G. (1966) 'The Brighton girls', *Humping My Bluey*; © The Estate of Graham McInnes. Reading 3.3: Davis, R. (2008) *Writing Dialogue for Scripts*, 2008, 3rd edn; Methuen Drama. Extract of poem on page 155: Duffy, C.A. (1990) 'Hometown', *The Other Country*; Anvil Press Poetry Ltd; © Carol Anne Duffy. Extract of poem on page 162: Szirtes, G. (2004) 'My father carries me across a field', *New and Collected Poems*, 2008; Bloodaxe Books. Poem on page 171: Dooley, M. (1986) 'Bathers 1930', *Explaining Magnetism*; Bloodaxe Books Ltd. Poem on page 174: Collins, B. (2001) 'Forgetfulness', *Sailing Alone Around the Room*; University of Pittsburgh Press. Poem on page 175: Laskey, M. (2008) 'The Lesson', *The Man Alone: New and Selected Poems*, 2008; Smith/Doorstop Books. Poem on pages 176–7: Hannah, S. (1995) 'Skipping rhyme for graduates', *The Hero and the Girl Next Door*; Carcanet Press Limited. Extract of poem on page 177: Used with permission of John Whitworth. Extract of poem on pages 178–9: by permission of Tony Harrison (*Selected Poems 2007* & *Collected Poems 2007* published by Penguin). Extract of poem on pages 179–80: Nimmo, D. (2000) 'Ill wishing him', The Wigbox: *New and Selected Poems*, 2000; Smith/Doorstop Books. Poem on pages 184–5: Hattersley, G. (1994) 'Spider', *Don't Worry*; Bloodaxe Books; used with permission of the author. Reading 4.1 Example 3: Lavery B (1987) 'Origin of the Species', Methuen, London; © 1987 by Bryony Lavery. Reading 4.2: Mitchell, J. (1976) *Amelia*; © Joni Mitchell. Reading 4.3: Draycott, J. (2009) 'Golf', *Over*, 2009; Carcanet Press Limited. Reading 4.4: Dharker, I. (2001)

'I Speak for the Devil 2001', Robertson Pearce, P. and Astley, N. *In Person: 30 Poets*; Bloodaxe Books Ltd. Reading 4.5: Murray, L. (1992) 'Shoal', *Translations from the Natural World*; Carcanet Press Limited.

Every effort has been made to contact copyright holders. If any have been inadvertently overlooked the publishers will be pleased to make the necessary arrangements at the first opportunity.

Index

Page numbers in **bold** type refer to figures